'Keep it simple, and God will not forsake you'
Life and teachings of St. Leo of Optina and St. Theodore of Neamts

Serge Jumati

Gozalov Books
The Hague

© Gozalov Books, The Hague, 2022
Publisher: Marijcke Tooneman
Telephone: +31703521565
E-mail: gozalovbooks@planet.nl
Website: www.hetsmallepad.nl

ISBN: 9789079889655; 978-90-79889-65-5
The English translation of a Russian book ΄Преподобный Лев Оптинский' by Serge Jumati.

Editors: Convent of the Mother of God Portaïtissa, Trazegnies, Belgium, portaitissa@skynet.be;
Gouri Gozalov
Translator: Gozalov Books
Proofreading: Nikolai Bot
Illustrations: Natali Komarovskaya
Cover image: drawing by Natali Komarovskaya "St. Leo"
Design: Guram Kochi

All rights reserved. No part of this publication may be reproduced or transmitted in any form or by any means, electronic or mechanical, including photocopy and recording, or stored in a retrieval system, without the written permission of the publisher.

Table of Contents

Publisher's Foreword 4
Chapter 1. Reviving of the Optina monastery 5
Chapter 2. Quenchless spiritual thirst 11
Chapter 3. New father superior of the Beloberezhsky
              monastery 16
Chapter 4. Schemamonk Theodore,
              mentor and teacher of father Leo 19
Chapter 5. Conflicts in the Balaam monastery 26
Chapter 6. A school of monasticism
              in the Svirsky monastery 34
Chapter 7. Spiritual mentor of the Optina monastery 42
Chapter 8. The history of the skete 44
Chapter 9. Working days in the skete 55
Chapter 10. Ill-feelings of some laity
              and Optina monks towards father Leo 64
Chapter 11. Life and Teaching of Father Leo 77
Chapter 12. Memories of father Leo
              by his spiritual children 87
Chapter 13. The last days of father Leo 96

Publisher's Foreword

This is a life story of two spiritual mentors in the Eastern Christian Orthodox tradition, St. Leo of Optina (Nagolkin) and St. Theodore of Neamts (Polzikov). St Theodore was a disciple of St. Paisios (Velichkovsky). St Paisios re-established in several monasteries on Athos and in Romania, where he was father superior, the practice of incessant prayer to Jesus Christ. This practice is known as 'Jesus prayer' and he had discovered this practice in the writings of ancient Christian ascetics.

St. Leo and St. Theodore established the schools of inner prayer and revelation of thoughts amongst the monks in Optina and several other monasteries at the end of the 18th – beginning of the 19th century. Inner prayer, revelation of thoughts and admonishing through acting, amongst other methods of purifying and elevating the soul for the sake of receiving the Holy Spirit, were almost forgotten by that time. In the life of the clergy the stress was put on the obedience to the superiors in the hierarchy, strict complying to the church rules and following church services and the work of penance. The inner core of the monks remained often untouched by this, they couldn't open it to the light of the Gospel.

St. Leo and St. Theodore had to endure the hostility of some church hierarchs and monks, who didn't understand the necessity of inner work on the way to God. They did it firmly but at the same time full of love for their fellowmen and revived the spiritual mentorship amongst the Eastern Orthodox Christian clergy as well as the laity.

Marijcke Tooneman
The Hague, september 2022

Chapter 1. Reviving of the Optina monastery

It was 1797. A man of giant stature and build went humbly through the gates of the Optina monastery of the Presentation in the Temple. His eyes gave away that he had an outstanding mind and inborn keenness of wit. His name was Leo Nagolkin, and he was 29 years old.

It was not idle curiosity or poverty that had led Leo to this dilapidated monastery, but the fire of ardent prayer, burning in his heart.

Until that time, Leo had lived and worked in the city of Bolhov, Orlov province. He had an education, but he had no means of livelihood, so Leo began as a shop assistant of the merchant Sokolnikov and began selling hemp and hemp oil. Thanks to his intelligence and wit, honesty and loyalty to the business of his boss his sales "took off". The money of the merchant was adding up, their trade expanded, and Leo could enjoy travelling to different cities of the province and Russia and contact with people from different social classes. It happened very seldom that anyone of the Bolhov merchants travelled outside the district to sell hemp, but he established contact with St. Petersburg merchants whom he also sold goods. For this he often had to travel to the city of Sukhinichi in the Kaluga province.

His splendid memory enabled him to be an excellent conversationalist. When conversing with him some took him for a fleet officer, others as belonging to the entourage of some nobleman, still others thought he was an industrialist, so freely could he speak about people with such lives and professions. Being constantly on the move and communicating with people, Leo gained a lot of knowledge of people, and experience.

All in all, the master grew rich moneywise and Leo mentally. Even a physical injury he received when he was travelling around on business could not disparage his firm step. And very few people knew that in the heart of the successful salesman, to whom the boss was going to give his daughter in marriage, flared the spark of love for God. This spark of love God had given to him. It gently and secretly protected him with prayers from the hurricane winds of passions that lead to the heights of earthly life. That's why he gave up this worldly happiness and crossed the threshold of the holy monastery.

We return to the beginning of the story. It was not curiosity, nor poverty that had led Leo to this dilapidated monastery, but the desire to take the monastic vow.

Leo did not even suspect that just two years ago the monastery had been on the verge of disappearing, that in 1724 the impoverished monastery had been abolished by a decree of the synod, that it had been attached to the Belyovsky Transfiguration monastery. That the monastery fences, buildings, farmyard, and all church utensils had been disassembled and transported to Belyov. That only thanks to benefactors of the monastery, namely nobleman

Shepelyov, they had managed to defend the monastery from total neglect and destruction.

We'll leave Leo inside the monastery walls for now and try to describe the life and rebirth of the Optina monastery at the time.

In 1795 the city Kozelsk and with it also Optina came under the jurisdiction of the Moscow eparchy. The metropolitan of Moscow and Kaluga, Plato, made a tour to inspect the monasteries and churches of the diocese. When he was in the Kaluga region, he saw the small stone church with a blue dome studded with golden stars on the other bank of the river Zhizdra behind a blackened pole fence. It was the church of the Presentation in the Temple. Nearby stood a few rickety wooden structures - cells, household rooms... The poor monastery with three elderly monks (one of them blind) could barely keep up a prayerful life. Everything was poor, darkish and cheerless. He felt a gripping pain in his heart and tears came to his eyes. "Let there be a monastery here," whispered his mouth inspired by the Holy Spirit. He stood there for a long time with a grieving heart, and he became firm in the decision he had taken.

When he had returned to Moscow, he invited the father superior of the Peshnoshsky monastery, archimandrite Makarios, and instructed him to visit the Optina monastery, to revive it and to put it in order. Father Makarios appointed Peshnoshsky priest-monk Joseph to oversee the monastery. But, after spending a year there as a father superior, father Joseph resigned as superior because of an illness. Metropolitan Plato turned to father Makarios a second time: "Choose from your brethren a man capable to fulfil this task, Optina must be revived and become a coenobitic monastery with a hard way of life." Father Makarios said, "But I have no such man, your eminence. Should I really give you the gardener Abraham?" His eminence felt this was a kind of strange slip of the tongue of father Makarios and that made him want to meet this gardener. Father Abraham had to come to Moscow. Out of humility father Abraham brought forth all kinds of arguments in an attempt to decline becoming superior: "...And I'm not healthy, and this assignment is far above my strength..." But whatever arguments father Abraham brought forth, vladyko was unbending: "You're not old, and God will give you strength. Bow to the inevitable and start to fulfil the service that I appointed you." And also, the mentors Samuel Golutvensky and John Peshnoshsky told him that this was the call of God, and... father Abraham set out for Optina.

He found the monastery in extreme desolation: "There wasn't even a towel for the servant to wipe his hands," said father Abraham, "and there was nothing to relieve the misfortune and poverty. I was just crying and praying, praying and crying." And also, the local Kozelsk people, soldiers and peasants caused many problems for the monastery. In his grief the father superior went to his spiritual mentor Makarios in Peshnosh to beg him to relieve him of his crushing burden. But father Makarios remembered the request of his eminence Plato to him not to leave Optina in trouble, so he ordered to harness horses to his cart and drove to an acquainted landowner taking father Abraham with him. "They," remembered father Abraham, "supplied me in a short time with everything necessary so that I brought two cartloads of various things to the monastery. Returning from collecting the loads, my mentor asked me to co-celebrate with him, and after the service and the common meal all of a sudden, he addressed the brotherhood with these words: "Fathers and brothers! To those who wish to go with father Abraham to build the monastery that he is entrusted with, I will not only put no obstacles in the way, but I will bless them with love to help this good cause." Several monks and workers volunteered to go to Optina. In the end there were in total 12 people.

About the offences committed by the local population against the monastery, father Abraham wrote a letter to metropolitan Plato in the hope he would bring the violators to justice:

"They steal wood, they are fishing without permission in the waters of the monastery, they cut brushwood, which is needed for the monastery itself, they come at night and mow the best grass in the monastery meadows. On the 7th of May they carried off a couple of monastery horses and although the thieves were caught, the Kozelsk authorities do not help the monastery at all: they protect those thieves. Again, in May, during the distribution of the residents' meadows for the cavalry, the Kozelsk authorities allotted also monastic meadows. In winter they ride through the monastery forest where a lot of trees were felled, near the very monastery. In summer they walk over our wood lots and sing so loudly that during the divine service it can be heard in the church. That's why we think that the former father superior, father Joseph, resigned. Not due to physical illness, but because of the emotional trouble that comes from this agitation. Because of this many of the novices left the monastery, while others intend to go away, and also on this account this monastery cannot be put in order as befits it." Under the petition were the signatures of hegumen Athanasius, the monks Parfenios and Ignatios, the novices Maxim, Gabriel, Michael, Onesimus, Yevstigney and Matthew.

Only a directive of governor Obleouhov at the request of metropolitan Plato put an end to the lawlessness committed by the local people.

Metropolitan Plato comforted the petitioners with the following resolution in response to the petition: "Holy monastic life prescribes to either avert all these misfortunes or overcome them with patience, and God will invisibly protect His servants if He sees their patience."

The number of monks began to grow rapidly. Father Makarios endorsed and supervised father Abraham.

"Most of all I want to ask you to love all the brethren equally. Those you intend to tonsure monk, put them to the test first. Then ask them before God whether their promise to be committed to you and the monastery is firm, whether they will not leave the monastery without asking your permission. And only then tonsure them. If you see that they want to only formally be tonsured, it is best not to take them. For each you will have to answer to God. The fewer the brethren, the less also will be the sorrow and confusion. May God give you and father Pimen spiritual love for each other and a clear conscience towards each other, then also the brotherhood will be peaceful." Thus, father Makarios wrote to father Abraham.

An exemplary internal order established itself in the monastery, the brethren endured want with Christian self-denial, prayerful trust in God and laborious obedience.

Such a monastery appeared before the eyes of Leo.

Chapter 2. Quenchless spiritual thirst

"Accept me into the monastery, father," Leo addressed himself to the father superior Abraham. Father Abraham looked intently at the young man standing in front of him. How could he not accept someone of blazing health, educated, with a keen and humble look? Leo spent two years in the Optina monastery as a novice. Two years of labours on the verge of his physical strength in humility and prayer.

The nephew of merchant Sokolnikov where Leo had worked as a shop-assistant, Maxim Sokolnikov, came to the monastery to be a novice along with Leo. Maxim was not inferior in strength to Leo. So, the two of them constantly amazed the brethren and the father superior with their feats of labour and brought significant savings to the empty treasury of the monastery as well. A bit urgently, just in one day it was necessary to connect two monastery lakes with a channel. To dig the channel in one day they would have to hire twenty people, provide them with tools, feed them during the day, and pay for the work at that. Leo and Maxim looked at each other, and they declared, for everybody to hear: we are up to that, in a day we will finish it. And to everyone's surprise, they finished the job just as they claimed, and their reward was 15 pounds of bread. With similar labours two years went by.

Of course, the daily liturgical cycle in the monastery was performed conscientiously under the constant supervision of father Abraham. But as father Abraham wrote to emperor Alexander Pavlovich: "The divine services are performed in dire need, and that ...causes noticeable sorrow to the worshippers." The monastery was in disorder, so the amount of heavy physical work was very big, which took away all strength. No doubt father Abraham had the gift of grace of the Holy Spirit. Otherwise, it would be impossible to explain how in 19 years he accomplished works that would normally take a century. He managed to save the monastery from destruction, organize monastic life according to the coenobitic statute, finish the construction of the three-tiered bell tower and stone cells for the brethren on both sides of it, build a stone refectory with a wooden entresol and the same kind of building for the rectory. Many buildings were erected, including the stone Kazan cathedral. A nobleman who lived in Optina, Alexey Tatischev cultivated a magnificent garden between the buildings with fruit trees and flowers. Father Abraham also achieved to increase the number of monks in the monastery from seven to thirty. Next to the monks there were a lot of workers in the monastery.

When you are troubled by thirst you drink a glass of water. When you are troubled by hunger you eat. But what do you do when you are tormented by spiritual thirst and hunger? Once you have tasted the sweetness of prayer, experienced the bliss of God's presence in the heart, you grow constantly hungry, you start to constantly look for satiation. His hunger to learn the spiritual life forced Leo to turn to father Abraham with the request to transfer him to the Beloberezhsky monastery. A then well-known ascetic was father superior there: spiritual mentor Basilios (Kishkin), who had lived for a long time on mount Athos together with the disciples of venerable Paisios (Velichkovsky). Leo received the blessing to transfer and in 1799 he went to the Beloberezhsky monastery. As a sprout from a seed makes its way through a thick layer of earth to the sun, thus also the soul of Leo made its way to the light of God through works of obedience and humility. Through the efforts of father Basilios and his disciples the monastic life had been set going here as well. Vigil was served here properly, it lasted for at least 7 hours. Father Basilios was a man of inner work, he had studied prayer of the heart, for which after the evening church rules, he went into the woods, where he had a cell. There he spoke in silence alone with the One God, and when night fell, he would come back to the monastery.

The establishment of peace and harmony between the brothers was his principal care, and where there is peace and harmony, there is Christ also. As for obedience, he gave them to everyone very felicitously. It often happened that the monks from gentry bore the burden of labours more patiently than those who were used to physical labours. Father Basilios himself liked physical work and appreciated it.

It sometimes happened that the brethren did not lock their cells when they set out to mow. In such cases father Basilios often went by the cells to see who was doing what and who needed what. During such a visit of his, he would sometimes leave there some consolation: bagels, cakes, a comb, and other things as required. And if a cell was filthy, littered, he cleaned and swept it, but afterwards he would explain that the monk's cell should be clean and tidy, and that "your guardian angel esteems your work." But most of all he advised to try to stay in the cell with fear of God, to do readings of the God-bearing fathers and to do the Jesus prayer in the mind as if stringing these words to the heart, to make bows to the ground only up to one's strength, but often and with affection. "When you go to bed imagine yourself lying in a coffin waiting, because "Behold, the groom is arriving" (Matthew 25:6), and you will be judged." That's the kind of father superior with whom Leo acquired experience in spiritual work.

In 1801 Leo was tonsured into the mantle with the name Leo and ordained a hierodeacon, and then a hieromonk. There were different kinds of coenobites in the monastery: some were totally unable to subdue their passions and would start to put forward all possible requirements to father Basilios, others kept silent, and only a few had humility in their heart. So, it happened once that upon the occurrence of a church holiday the brethren who performed obedience in the choir refused to perform the service because they were unhappy with something. In this way they hoped to force the father superior to fulfil some of their demands. But the abbot did not want to give in to them and to humble them he called father Leo and another brother to sing the festive service. Father Leo had driven hay from the farm all day. He was tired and covered with dust, and he was just going to take a rest, when he was told the will of the father superior. Without any grumbling he went to the church and together with his comrade they sang the vespers and matins. Another occurrence shows the great kindness of father Leo. In the desert there was a brother who had fallen to delusions. Once, he went up the bell tower and cried: "Look! See! When I fall, I won't get smashed up, angels of God will carry me in their hands!" Father Leo was at that time working on an obedience. When he heard the hysterical screams of his brother, he abandoned his work and ran to the bell tower. He only just managed to grab the edge of the clothes of his brother gone mad who leaned over the balustrade and was sliding down. Since he had enough strength, he could hold the man hanging in the air and keep him from falling. Then he pulled him inside the bell tower. Father Leo not only saved him from death, but also looked after the soul of his brother who had almost perished: He made clear to him he had been deluded.

Monastery walls and black robes do not save you from your passions. After all, also demons might help you pray. As soon as the slightest idea of being chosen, the slightest idea about you being different from other people visits your mind, consider that you have already embarked on the path of perdition. The pronoun "I", "I", "I" itself is the root of our vanity. Is it not better to say: "The Lord helped me...", "My spiritual father gave me..."?

What reason prompted father Leo to temporarily move to the Cholnsky monastery is unknown. But we know that it is there, where father Leo met his future mentor and teacher schemamonk Theodore, a former disciple of the great spiritual mentor Paisios (Velichkovsky), father superior of the Moldovlachian monasteries. Many monks of the Cholnsky monastery profited from the spiritual guidance of father Theodore who was experienced in the ascetic life and had the grace of the Holy Spirit. But father Leo clung to him with all his soul.

Chapter 3. New father superior of the Beloberezhsky monastery

"As easily as someone gets lost on his way if he has no guide, even if he is very clever, just as easily someone gets lost if he goes the path of monasticism self-willedly, even if he has all wisdom."

In 1804, hegumen Basilios left his position as father superior at the Beloberezhsky monastery. Someone had to be elected to take his place. All the monastic brethren gathered together, and they began to discuss who should be elected as father superior. "They can choose someone also without my presence," thought father Leo, and he went to brew kvass. The brotherhood deliberated for a long time and came to the unanimous conclusion that apart from father Leo there was no one else to choose. All together they came to the kvass brewery and announced their decision to father Leo. According to his humility father Leo did not go against the decision of the brothers but changed his clothes and went with them to bishop Dositheus in Oryol. Bishop immediately approved the decision of the brotherhood. That's how monk Leo became father superior of the Beloberezhsky monastery. However, the authoritative position of father Leo did not change his simple way of life. His precept: "Keep it simple and God will not forsake you" was his breath of life. So, if work compelled him to go somewhere, he went with one horse, in a simple cart and without a coachman. One day hieromonk Gabriel, a native of Karachevsky, turned to father Leo with the request to visit his birthplace. This was after the chirotony of Gabriel. "If the need arises to go there for monastery affairs, I'll let you know," said father Leo. The opportunity to go to those territories soon presented itself. "Father Gabriel! Get ready," father Leo called father Gabriel to prepare for the journey. Father Gabriel had already made every effort. He had prepared to visit his relatives

gloriously: he had carefully packed his festive cassock and kamelaukion in a special hatbox. He thought he'd come in full dress to impress his relatives so to speak with his festive appearance. But imagine his disappointment! The hour of departure had come. They prayed to God, went out. Father Gabriel saw that they were given a cart with a front seat, drawn by a single horse. "Where's the driver?" asked father Gabriel. "What?" the father superior was surprised. "It is the habit...," said father Gabriel. Father Leo replied: "So that I have three drivers for one horse? Thank you! Why don't you sit down, brother, on the front, and if you get tired, I'll sit there. And what's this? A hat box and cassock? Well, I myself do not take my kamelaukion with me... But you, if you take your ceremonial dress with you, then you sit down at my place, and I will drive the horse."
Immediately he sat down on the front. The confused father Gabriel was no longer glad he had taken his ceremonial dress. He took it to his cell at once and asked the father superior to take his place, and he himself took the place of the coachman. That's how easily father Leo corrected the pernicious intention of father Gabriel. Life in the monastery flowed in measured steps. Father Leo followed the statutes of monastic life, appointed obedience, led the worship, and spiritually nourished the brethren.
After some time, schemamonk Theodore[1] knocked at the gate of the monastery. Envy on the part of the brotherhood of the Cholnsky monastery about his spiritual dispensation had forced Theodore to leave the Cholnsky monastery and go to the Beloberezhsky monastery. Naturally he was glad to see that the father superior of the Beloberezhsky

1 Schemamonk Theodore formerly helped father superior Paisios (Velichkovsky) with his translations in the Neamts monastery. In Russia he lived in different monasteries and often suffered persecution for receiving other monks "to reveal their intentions", i.e. for spiritual guidance which was still unknown in Russian monasteries, even in Balaam (†1822, Svirsky monastery) [Russian church history, prof. P.V. Znamensky]

monastery was father Leo, with whom he became close spiritually when he lived in the Cholnsky monastery. But father Leo was even more pleased to meet his teacher. Yes, how couldn't he rejoice? The soul has no nerves, and when it is deadly sick, smitten with the sores of sins, a dying man cannot feel he is dying. He cannot even see his sins. Father Leo clearly understood that no one is more unfortunate and closer to perdition than someone who has no mentor on the path to God. He gladly accepted the spiritual guidance of mentor Theodore.

Chapter 4. Schema monk Theodore, mentor and teacher of father Leo

For four years father Leo was father superior of the Beloberezhsky monastery. In 1807 a fever was brought to Belye Berega.[2] Many monks were infected by it. Schemamonk Theodore, an ardent admirer of Jesus' life-giving commandments, mercifully cared for them. To strengthen his zealot the Lord also let him to become ill, and during his illness he announced to him through an angel, that no enemies' machinations can harm his soul. He grew very weak and for nine days he didn't eat anything. Everyone thought that the hour of death had come for the righteous man. All of a sudden, he lost his senses, his eyes were open and constantly remained in the same position, his breathing was barely noticeable, his body became numb, his lips lit up with a paradisiacal smile, a blush began to play on his face. For three days he remained in this unusual state, and then he woke up. Father Leo came running. "Father! Are you dying?" "No," answered Theodore, "I will not die, I was told that. Look, were there ever dying people with such strength? And with those words he gave him a hand. His favourite pupil hieromonk Gabriel came running. "I considered you to be great, but God showed me that you are very small," Theodore said to him to teach him and for his own good. He was enthralled and strengthened by Divine inner ardour, so after that he got out of bed, and only in his shirt, leaning on a crutch, supported by disciples, he rushed to the aid of his neighbour. Evidently something had been disclosed to him during his illness. We have no words to recount spiritual things, they can only be indicated with allegories. A few days before his illness, in the evening, when he reconciled his disciple with the father superior, father Leo, he felt in his heart an extraordinary consolation. He was unable to contain the sweetness and

2 Belye Berega. Village in the Bryansk province. (tr.)

he began to hint about his elevated experience to father Leo. The disease itself progressed strangely: during his illness father Theodore was in full possession of his faculties, but his face gave away the strong inner action of prayer. He could sense heat in his body, and he felt moderately weak. Then his soul soared out of his body and some invisible youth appeared. He could feel him with his heart. The youth took him by a narrow road to the left. "I have already passed away," thought father Theodore, "no one knows, shall I be saved, or shall I perish?" "You are saved!" replied a voice, and suddenly some force, similar to a rapid vortex took him and moved him to the right. 'Try the sweetness of heavenly betrothals, which I give to those that love Me,' said an invisible voice to him. With these words, he thought the Saviour Himself put His right hand on his heart, and he was enraptured by an unspeakably pleasant abode, invisible, ineffable by words in earthly language. And from this feeling he moved to another even more magnificent feeling, and then to a third, both of which, in his own words, he could remember only with his heart, he could not understand them with his mind. 'Then I saw a church, and in it on the right side, close by the altar I saw a hut in which there were five or six people. For these people, your death will be revoked, for them you will still live,' said the mental voice. Then the spiritual age of some of his disciples was revealed to him. Finally, the Lord announced to him the temptations that he will have to endure. He even saw the persons, who will direct their malice against him. But the divine voice assured him that the ship of the soul cannot be harmed by these ferocious waves, because the invisible ruler of this is Christ.

In a short time, without medication, mentor Theodore recovered. He desired to live a more solitary and silent life, and he spoke about this to the father superior, father Leo. The brotherhood built a cell in the forest for him, about two and a half kilometres from the monastery. He moved there together with hieroschemamonk Cleophas. In order not to part from father Theodore father Leo resigned as father superior in 1808, and he also moved near to father Theodore. In a solitary cell father Leo was tonsured into the schema with the name Leo. Father Theodore sometimes jokingly referred to his fellow as "the humble lion".

Soon the fame of the great virtues of schemamonk Theodore spread far and wide. Countless visitors constantly crowded at the doors of his cell, and they broke the silence of the hermitage's dwellers. Father Theodore and his fellow labourers grew weary of the rumour, prayed unto the Lord, telling in the prayer about the gravity of their situation: "O Lord! Arrange our affairs according to Thy holy will." For three years they were forced to put up with the spiteful glares and words of some of the brothers and the father superior of the monastery. But the path full of hardship, sorrow and oppression was just beginning for them. Providence determined for father Theodore to leave Belye Berega before his comrades. The hermitage of father Theodore burned down. Then father Theodore decided to go to the Novoezersky monastery, which was in the eastern part of the province of Novgorod, and the head of which was the then famous Theophanes.

A lover of non-possession, he took just thirty kopecks with him on the road, a gift of the Svensky hegumen. Athanasius, one of his devoted schemamonks, secretly put a five-rouble banknote in his pocket to ease the way. Athanasius knew the contempt the righteous man had for money; a contempt born from his strong confidence in God. But after walking sixty versts from Belye Berega Theodore met an elderly beggar woman, and gladly he gave her these five roubles. Archimandrite Theophanes took him in lovingly and proposed to him to revive the Nilo-Sorskaya hermitage and live in it with his companions. But for this it was necessary to obtain a permit from metropolitan Ambrose. The metropolitan did not agree to the proposal of archimandrite Theophanes, and sent father Theodore to the Paleostrovsky hermitage, which lies on the northern part of the island in lake Onega. God's providence was behind everything.

Here providence tried father Theodore in a fire of cruel temptations. We do not always dwell on mount Tabor: Golgotha is indispensable. A path on which we would meet with nothing but spiritual delights without experiencing any grief would be a path leading to downfall. Father Theodore's guide was his humility. Humility is acquired by diligent fulfilment of the commandments of the Lord, when we realize that we are infirm by nature, because of our human characteristics. Humility is to wholeheartedly put oneself in the hands of God, it is inner poverty in spirit, according to the first of the beatitudes. When you read what father Theodore had to endure you will become firmly convinced of the idea that God gave him such an abundance of humility that he became totally unsusceptible to the malice of people. Their malice burnt up in father Theodore's love of God and people, a love enveloping him like a fire.

The father superior of the Paleostrovsky monastery was Belousov. By birth he was of the merchant class. First, he bought nobility, then monkhood. He did not grasp the commandments of a true Christian and of monasticism. He blazed in envy of father Theodore, and he began to oppress him. But his abuse of power as father superior alone could not satiate his anger. Belousov collected various libels against the chaste schemamonk, and with them he presented himself to the metropolitan. What father Theodore had to endure in this monastery is best described by himself:

"On the 19th February 1811 the father superior returned to the monastery with an order from his eminence metropolitan Ambrose, in which, among other things, the following was said: 'Schemamonk Theodore should not be let out, not participate in any monastic activities, and if he does anything indecent, anything contrary to his rank, then his rank should be withdrawn and he should be sent to the secular team.'" This was read during the meal, and besides that Belousov forbade the virtuous mentor to enter the cells of other monks, to let them into his own cell and talk to pilgrims. "All of this happened," said humble Theodore, "because of my grave sins, my pride, and my loose tongue. Glory to Thee, merciful creator of mine and God, that You do not leave me, a great and bad sinner, but visit me and punish me for my transgressions by Your generosity and fatherly mercy!!!"

On February 26th father Theodore asked permission to submit a request to the Balaam monastery, but he was refused. "Clearly," he said, "it so pleases the merciful God: Blessed be the name of the Lord from henceforth and forever!"

March 20th a new decree was sent in which was written: "Don't let schemamonk Theodore out of the gates of the monastery to go anywhere, he is only allowed to go out to collect firewood and water." "Merciful Lord and creator of mine," said Theodore, "Give to me that I may stand this and what henceforth may happen because of my sins with thanksgiving and placidity through the prayers of my fathers. Without Your help I cannot do anything good, let me at least make a beginning to live my life according to Your holy will from now, and to love Thee, my merciful God, creator and redeemer!!!"

On the 4th of August 1811 the father superior Joseph urged him to go on an obedience, to rake hay. "Since the decree I may not go out," replied Theodore. Father Joseph got angry and said, "I'll put you in the cellar, and I'll give you only grass to eat!" "Do as you please," said Theodore, "but I have faith in my merciful God, people may only do to me what He allows because of my sins. And I wish it myself. It is better for me to be punished in this age than to be eternally tormented in the age to come. And they reproached me," writes father Theodore, "for getting firewood and water with their blessings. And now, with the help of God, I suppose I will not go out of the gates of the monastery at all anymore, but merciful God, only help me wretched sinner."

August 22nd, 1811. "Father superior Joseph kept urging me to go out to get shoes, and I told him that I could not go out.

He got worked up because of that answer and scolded me very much. Among other things he said: 'I know what you want,' and I answered: 'Thank God that you were favoured with insight.' And he got angry and shouted: 'Chain this son of a bitch up!' and he was about to hit me on the cheek, but because of the prayers of my fathers he did not hit me, but said: 'I will tell all about you, son of a bitch, to the metropolitan, so that you will never again get out of your cell, or else I will nail down your doors.' Glory to Thee merciful creator and God that You punish me, a great and bad sinner, for my transgressions."

"On August 26th our father superior said to father Jacob: 'When Theodore does not join the common meal, then give him only bread and kvass.' Let Thy steadfastness support this, Lord, and strengthen me, a big sinner who is almost too feeble to do this. It is better for me, with Thy help, Lord, to endure poverty than to flout the holy apostles and the holy fathers and violate the rules."

"On September 2nd I begged our father superior Joseph to let me leave the monastery or allow me to file a request. But he only reproached me for my faint-heartedness and said that there is no God in the faint-hearted. And however, many times I asked him, I could see from his words, that there was no hope to obtain mercy from him. Merciful Lord and creator of mine, render me help according to Thy ways and arrange our fates as You want and as is useful for my sinful soul."

For two years the harassments from the side of the father superior continued, for two years father Theodore was deprived of clothing and footwear. The steadfast father Theodore thus earned the crowns of patience. Finally, when he saw that the abnormality of the Paleostrovsky monastery was incurable and the hatred of the father superior irreconcilable, father Theodore decided to go to the metropolitan to explain himself personally... But father Theodore did not find understanding in the metropolitan, and therefore he left the monastery without permission and went to the Balaam monastery.

At the same time when father Theodore was in a crucible where human passions are burnt, father Leo and father Cleophas built a new cell in the place where the hermitage cell had burnt down. They hoped to continue a solitary ascetic life. But there came no end to the stream of brethren from the monastery that came to them for spiritual nourishment and laity that turned to them for advice. The father superior did not like the external disarray of the monastic way of life. So, he sent a report to bishop Dositheus. Bishop Dositheus however did not make any inquiry. He wanted to reassure the father superior with his dictate, so he ordered father Leo to leave the Beloberezhsky monastery, adding to it that "two wolves do not live in one den".

Chapter 5. Conflicts in the Balaam monastery

In the year 1811 father Leo, father Cleophas and a disciple of father Leo, monk Amphilochios, moved to live in the Balaam monastery. By God's providence soon also father Theodore made it to the Balaam monastery. They began to live together in a monastic skete. However, for leaving the Paleostrovsky monastery without permission father Theodore was forbidden to wear the kamelaukion for a year. "Glory to our merciful God," wrote father Theodore shortly after his arrival in Balaam to father Athanasius, "that He has granted also me, unworthy as I am, to live with my fathers in the Balaam skete. Already now we cannot make any excuse nor find any justification before our merciful Creator and Redeemer. He has fulfilled our whole desire... Indeed, we can boast of the mercy of God that has been shown to us, unworthy as we are. He has led us to a place silent, peaceful, remote from people, free of common talk. Father Leo was appointed supervisor in our skete. Now we must only pray to the merciful God that He will give that from now on we will make a start to love Him and live according to His holy will and keep His divine commandments."

The Balaam brotherhood still did not have its own experienced teachers at that time. They soon realized what a treasure they had been sent by the providence of God in the mentors. Their stay in Balaam was the beginning of spiritual mentorship in this ancient monastery, which from then on flourished with a whole host of its own zealots. Soon the cell of the three spiritual mentors became a true centre of the spiritual life of Balaam. Among those who came for spiritual guidance from father Theodore and father Leo there was the cellarer of the Balaam monastery father Eudocimus, confessor of the monastery. First, he went through monastic life without a spiritual instructor. He thought to achieve spiritual perfection by external deeds and perfect obedience to his father superior alone. He considered himself the pupil of the father superior, hegumen Innocent. However, neither obedience, up to readiness to die at the precept of the father superior, nor external exploits brought him significant fruits of monastic life. Father Eudocimus found in himself neither meekness, nor humility, nor tears, nor love. All he saw was the dryness and cruelty of his soul, and how filled it was with passions. Because of this he had lost his inner peace. He was at a loss: "After all, I fulfil all you have to do when you follow the patristic writings and advice of experienced people." It reached the point that he fell into despair, and evil thoughts led him to plan to commit suicide by jumping off a cliff into the bay. But the Lord inspired him to give up all sorts of high opinions about his righteousness and turn to father Theodore and father Leo.

They revealed to him in their conversations that work and bodily exercises do not lead by itself to progress, on the contrary, they cause growing of pride and vanity, and as a consequence - to callousness, reproachfulness and to a sad end, which is despair. Without the inner, humble, secret work of prayer, next to considering yourself the worst of all, we cannot soften, submit ourselves, and feel a childlike evangelical joy. Father Leo and father Theodore showed him the true key that unlocks the heart. Although father Eudocimus was a monk mainly outwardly, he was a sincere monk. He understood that spiritual guidance is indispensable on the way of salvation. He became humble, revived and gradually calmed down. The number of visitors to the fathers Theodore and Leo grew even more.

But the numerous visitors disturbed the measured rhythm of life of the monastery. Some received great spiritual benefit from the advice and guidance from the mentors, but others, even sensible hermits, looked at the life of the mentors with perplexity, and even with reproach. For example, father Barlaam. He saw the truly ascetic life of the mentors and tried to follow them, but he was troubled by the fact that they were almost constantly among people.

"Father!" he asked father Leo, "I lapse into temptation because of you. How can it be that you are chatting and talking for days with worldly people? What is the use of this?"

"Brother, what an odd fellow you are," replied father Leo. "By the way, out of love of my neighbour I would talk to him for two days if needed for the benefit of his soul. And I won't lose inner balance."

Also, the devil did not slumber. Since such spiritual mentorship had been almost forgotten since the last century, people turned up who incited displeasure against the mentors. Unfortunately, hegumen Innocent, who was father superior of the Balaam monastery then, lapsed into temptation against the mentors. Their activities seemed to him to interfere with his governance of the monastery. After all, father Eudocimus, saved by following the instructions of father Leo, had been considered before to be the close disciple of the hegumen... Also, other brethren of Balaam Monastery appealed to father Leo for guidance. So, father superior Innocent found himself abandoned and held in contempt by the brothers, while he believed that he should be the only spiritual mentor in the monastery. The teaching of father Theodore and father Leo seemed to him some innovation. His dissatisfaction with the state of affairs in the monastery intensified when the minister of religious affairs, prince A.N. Golitsyn, who came to Balaam, spent all his time in the cell of father Theodore and father Leo. He even ordered tea for himself to be prepared in their cell and he invited the father superior of the monastery, father Innocent there. Father Innocent considered this as a damage to his personal credibility and filed a complaint to the metropolitan of Novgorod and St. Petersburg Ambrose about father Leo and father Theodore. He reckoned they disturbed the peace in the monastery. Metropolitan Ambrose knew the father superior of Balaam from his good side, as an honest and hard-working ascetic, and he was prejudiced against father Leo and father Theodore, and he was ready to bring charges against them. Rumours began to spread in the monastery that they wanted to expel father Theodore from the monastery, because he had been tonsured a monk not in Russia, but in Moldova... that he was just a burgher from Karachevsky and such. Father Leo did not stay clear of trouble either. However, the metropolitan instructed the assistant bishop, father Hilarion, supervisor of the district monasteries and father superior of the Konevsky monastery (who later became the archimandrite of Tikhvin) to investigate this matter. In February 1817 father Hilarion came to the Balaam monastery. To determine the essence of the matter he suggested that father Leo and father Theodore would answer thirty questions in writing. Father Hilarion was amazed when he read their answers, and later he said that he had never read such answers before.[3] He found their seemingly "disorderly conduct" higher than human wisdom. Father Hilarion tried to reconcile the father superior with them. Concurrently prince Golitsyn sent his fiduciary, A.N. Nikolsky, to Balaam. He had to inquire further into the matter and to encourage a reconciliation between the father superior and father Leo and father Theodore. On top of everything, a monk who was fond of them wrote about their troubles in the monastery to the two archimandrites in St. Petersburg, Filaret and Innocent. Later archimandrite Filaret became metropolitan of Moscow and archimandrite Innocent became bishop of Penza. They all took an active part in the conflict around the spiritual mentors by appearing before metropolitan Ambrose. The answer from father Hilarion about the innocence of the mentors also arrived just in time. The metropolitan saw with great distress that he had almost done a great injustice. Father superior Innocent was summoned by metropolitan. Metropolitan received him

---

[3] Later venerable hegumen of Optina Isaac (Antimonov) sought these answers when he was compiling the lives of mentors Theodore and Leo. He sent a request to the Balaam monastery to father superior Damaskin, but his search was unsuccessful.

sternly: "What did you, old fool, do to me? By your fault I almost sentenced people who are better than you and I." The father superior was punished, the fathers Leo and Theodore had to be left in peace and cared for in every way, with the threat that, if any complaint from them will be heard, he would be replaced. The mentors were told they could be confident in the protection of the highest authorities.

Of course, this was contrary to the monastic principles of the mentors. They could not assent to even the slightest suspicion they were to be preferred to the father superior, whose will every true monk of the monastery considers the expression of God's will. Knowing the human heart well, the fathers did not hope that the father superior was fully reconciled with such a situation. And they made the only right decision: to leave Balaam. The righteous life of the father superior Innocent, and the memory he has left have shown that this had only been an unfortunate misunderstanding, a temptation to which he had succumbed.

This sorrowful page in the life of father Leo was of great importance to him. It strengthened his faith and patience. He clearly saw that any true preacher of the Word of God cannot avoid suppression by people, but that persecution caused by man's wickedness is nought before Divine providence. It was then that he fastened in his decision to endure any slander and hatred with which he would meet in the course of his life, as it indeed happened later in Optina.

Father Leo came to St. Petersburg to meet metropolitan Ambrose to personally explain the temptations that had befallen him and father Theodore, and to ask for permission to change their place of residence. After he had registered himself at the metropolitan office, father Leo went to visit the nephew of father Theodore, monk Joannicios, who was candle bearer in the Alexander Nevsky Lavra. At this time Joannicios helped a parishioner, an acquaintance, the widow of colonel Cherkasov, Aquilina

Cherkasov. After her husband's death she lived with her sick daughter, Liubov. Over time her grief about her husband became an obsession. She passionately wanted to see him and feel him. Then the enemy of the mankind made his move. He arranged it so that she did not only start to see her dead husband, but also started to talk to him. When father Leo learned from father Joannicios about Cherkasov's delusionary condition, he visited her at her modest house in the garden of the parish deacon, where she moved in with her daughter because of her miserable situation. With God's help he healed her from delusion and planted in her the right beliefs concerning souls that have departed from this world. Her dreams stopped soon. But she had been left a widow, and when she had spent all her fortune, she had had to pawn her jewels at the bank. She had accumulated a big bundle of mortgage tickets. "When father Leo and father Joannicios visited me," told Aquilina Cherkasov, "I unintentionally took these tickets from the chest of drawers and put them down in front of them. I did not say a word. Father Leo silently pulled them closer to him and began to examine them. Then he lowered his head. We were scared, we thought maybe something had happened to him. But after a few minutes he uttered a moan: 'Oh, poor thing! You are to perish alive.' 'What does all that mean?' I cried. 'Or else,' father replied, 'you have to pay interest on these tickets, and if you don't, then they will add interest on interest; then all your stuff will have to go on sale, and if it is not enough, then you'll have to pay the remainder. The bank will not take less for what is theirs. And for a trifle you will sit in the debtor's prison, or simply in jail.' 'Oh, father, what should I do?' 'This is what you should do:' he said. He took a ticket and continued: 'You have to buy back this thing and sell it and use the proceeds to buy back another, and also sell and so on.'" To address this matter Diomede Kondratyev was invited, a freedman of K. Saltykov, who respected and loved father Leo. He punctually carried out everything suggested by father Leo, so much so that Cherkasov was soon freed of all debt interest payments. After that she began to receive a pension for herself and her sick daughter because she had been a pupil at the Smolny institute[4]. Thus, although she was in a very awkward position, she was spared the great misfortune that awaited her. In the house of the deacon, the owner of the outhouse, an apartment was vacated. He offered her to move out of the outhouse, which was located in the garden, to the apartment. But she refused, saying that she was happy there. Less than a quarter of an hour went by and father Leo with father Joannicios came in. Cherkasov relayed the offer of father deacon to them. At this father Leo says, "And it is exactly for this that I came to you. Move to the new apartment right now. Call father deacon!" Cherkasov asked to postpone the matter until tomorrow, but father Leo insistently said: "No, move now or never." When they called father deacon, they took workers who carried the belongings from the garden apartment to the apartment in the yard. And the owner of the outhouse locked the shutters and doors.

In the morning father deacon came to Cherkasov and said, "What's the source of all this, did God send you a guardian angel?" "Why?" she asked him. "Well, if you had stayed the night in the old apartment," continued the deacon, "you would have been killed. It turns out that the doors and the shutters of the bedroom window are broken, and therefore you would certainly have been killed." It soon became known that the intruders had been led by a former servant of the Cherkasov. They were caught while committing another crime, and they admitted this violation as well. The leader of this gang was killed during the arrest, but no one knew about this yet then. And Cherkasov told father Leo that their servant was a faithful and good man, the best of servants. To which father Leo said, "Oh! That was the last that was ever seen of him." "But surely he's still alive?" asked Aquilina Ivanovna. "No, his blood has already

---

[4] The Smolny institute for noble girls. A finishing school founded in 1754. [tr.]

gone through judgment,[5] all we can do is pray for him." A few days later the wife of the deceased told all that has been described here in detail to Cherkasov.

In June 1817, when father Leo and father Theodore had settled all their affairs in St. Petersburg and had received permission to leave Balaam, they moved to Alexander-Svirsky monastery. Father Cleophas who lived with them in the skete in Balaam died May 19th, 1816, and he was buried in the church near the altar.

---

[5] His blood has already gone through judgment. I.e. his body has already been punished. [tr.]

Chapter 6. A school of monasticism in the Svirsky monastery

In June 1817 schemamonk Theodore and hieroschemamonk Leo settled in the Alexander Svirsky monastery. They founded a "school of monasticism" there and began to teach the monks the wisdom of monastic obedience. Father Theodore was very strict with himself and strict with his disciples as well. He ate once a day, never drank tea, never locked his cell. He had only one shirt which he washed twice a year and he wore it until it was completely decaying. He covered himself with a piece of cloth when he was sleeping. When he would go to church, he put on a muhajjar (cotton fabric mixed with wool) cassock, a riason and a klobuk[6]. He didn't accept any gifts of anyone except for books, but he gave them to the monastery sacristy, and only after that he took them to read, when they were already public property. He fulfilled/carried on/executed his prayer rule in his cell and he was constantly engaged in prayer of the heart. He watched his disciples very strictly and if he would notice anyone of them had something he could do without, he gave it to someone else, or he replaced it with something of a worse quality. For example, he saw once his disciple with a beautiful prayer beads. He took it away from him and gave it to the monastery and gave him a rope with knots instead. Quite often in the summer he and his disciples were sent into the woods to pick berries. This was a task given by the monastery superiors. Without the permission of father Theodore no one dared to eat a single berry. If someone disobeyed him in this matter just three times, he would exclude him from his guidance. Also, father Theodore was wearing fetters. Father Theodore confessed to his spiritual friend father Leo, although he was father's Leo spiritual mentor. "Well, Leo, make sure you don't spare me," he would say when he started to confess. Together

---
[6] Klobuk. Headgear of an orthodox monk. [tr.]

with father Leo father Theodore wrote a number of letters to his spiritual disciples, especially to father Joannicios, his nephew. They wrote about the necessity to read the works of holy fathers, like venerable Isaac the Syrian, Cassian the Roman, John of the Ladder, and to be in obedience. They advised father Joannicios not to be self-willed and not to leave the territory of the monastery.

In 1820, the emperor travelled all over his northern domain. His path ran near the Alexander-Svirsky monastery. Father Theodore and father Leo foresaw the emperor would come. They humbly suggested to their superior, father archimandrite, to prepare to meet him, although this monastery was not designated in the itinerary of the emperor. The father superior accepted the proposal and at the time the emperor was scheduled to pass through he waited for him at the gates. Meanwhile the emperor was on his way and as usual he inquired after the locality and its inhabitants. Sometimes he himself asked the driver, sometimes he enquired through his coachman Elijah. When they approached the road where there was a cross to indicate the vicinity of the monastery and the road to follow, the emperor asked, "What is this cross for?" Upon learning that the Svirsky monastery was close by he ordered to go there, and he began to ask what kind of monastery it was and what kind of brotherhood there was. The driver, who went there quite often, replied that it was now better than before. "How come?" asked the emperor. "Recently the mentors father Theodore and father Leo settled there, and now also the church choir sings better and overall there is more order." The emperor who had heard these names from prince Golitsyn wished to meet them. He had heard they had been tried by tribulations. Meanwhile, the monastery was awaiting the emperor. When they drove up to the monastery the emperor was surprised at the reception. "Were you really waiting for me?" The father superior replied that he went out to meet him at the advice of the mentors. The emperor went into church to venerate the relics of venerable Alexander. The emperor in his humility wished to receive the blessing of the hieromonks and he bade they would not pull away their hands when he kissed them. Then he asked: "But where are father Theodore and father Leo?" The mentors came forward a bit, but to all questions they answered the emperor reservedly and briefly. The emperor noticed this and stopped his questioning. He thought they were inappropriate to ask inside the church. Still, he wished to receive father Theodore's blessing. "I can't bless you as I am a simple monk," said the humble mentor, "I'm just a peasant." The emperor politely excused himself and left to continue his journey.

One and a half years before his death father Theodore fell seriously ill and half a year before his death he could no longer get up from his bed. In 1822 the metropolitan of Gelati Euthymios was sent from Georgia to the monastery. As a former bishop he was lodged there in retirement. Metropolitan came to love father Theodore as a friend. Once, during the severe illness of father Theodore, he and archimandrite Gregory (also sent from Georgia) have been standing for an hour in the cold yard to pick the right time to talk to him, so as not to disturb his rest. When father Theodore came to and heard about the humility of the hierarch, he had to cry. He called him, and after having received his blessing, he said: "Your eminence, I will be your forerunner in blissful eternity." The gift of clairvoyance especially showed itself in father Theodore when his death drew near. "Oh, Theodore is great!" metropolitan Euthymios used to exclaim often.

Shortly before his death father Theodore answered questions one of his disciples. He strictly advised to keep to communal life, to avoid unnecessary communication, to observe moderation and simplicity in dress and footwear, to attend all the services and to the common meal, "to always remember God, i.e., to always have the Jesus prayer on the lips and in the mind," to constantly confess and often to receive communion.

In the Holy Week of 1822, the suffering of the patient intensified. Then father Theodore asked father Leo to read him the Gospel of Matthew, the last conversation of the Saviour with His disciples. The Lord gave him new strength. "I thought I would celebrate Easter already elsewhere, not with you," father Theodore said to his disciples, "but it pleases God to once again illuminate me, a worthless person, here on earth, with the life-giving resurrection of Christ. Glory to God, glory to God for everything! You also, give thanks to the Lord for my sufferings, for they take away from me a formidable burden of sins... I see finally the shore of the sea of life on which hitherto as a fragile boat my soul has been carried along by a storm of adversities. Fathers of mine!" he said turning to his disciples. "For the sake of the Lord, don't separate from each other, at the present most miserable time you can find but a few with whom you can breathe a word in good conscience." On Tuesday of the Bright Week, he felt particularly bad. In the evening he wanted milk. The next day he again enjoyed milk, but on the third day he refused, in order that the use of dairy "would not turn into a habit".

On April 7th in the evening archimandrite Makarios bade father Theodore farewell with the mystery of holy unction and he gave him holy communion. The monk's face lit up. It was the ninth hour. He was silent as if he was busy contemplating the heavenly world. Then he gave up his ghost with a gentle sigh. Although he had died his face retained the imprint of unearthly glory. "Reverential fear, sadness, joy and wonder suddenly seized the feelings of the disciples: they clearly read on the forehead of their spiritual father, that his soul with delight had flown out into the arms of luminous angels."

On the death of father Theodore metropolitan Euthymius arranged the burial at his own expense and received the brethren on the ninth day, and on the fourteenth day he piously passed away, too, joining in spiritual union with his friend.

Father Leo was left alone. But he continued to spiritually nourish the monks as he had done together with father Theodore. Among the disciples of father Leo was also Dimitry Brianchaninov, the future bishop Ignatius. Dimitry Brianchaninov entered the Alexander-Svirsky Monastery in obedience to father Leo in the twenty-first year of his life after having overcome many obstacles. Unquestioning obedience and deep humility characterised the behaviour of novice Brianchaninov. He devoted himself wholeheartedly under the spiritual guidance of father Leo and from the outset their relationship was notable for its sincerity and directness. The novice obeyed the will of his spiritual father in all; all his questions and misunderstandings were resolved directly by father Leo. Father Leo was not too lazy to reprimand his young pupil; he guided him on the path of outer and inner humility. With regard to Dimitry an extremely humbling kind of guidance was undertaken, most likely to overcome in the young academic and officer all the arrogance and self-importance which are usually characteristic of noble and educated men joining an environment of unsophisticated people. Father Leo constantly exposed his disciple to tests. The relationship between staretz Leo and his novice Ignatius was not simple at all. More about this can be read in the life of Ignatius Brianchaninov.

After the death of father Theodore, father Leo and his disciples decided to go to a more secluded place. About this decision he wrote to hieromonk P.: "It pleased you to write that in the present most poor times it seems we all need to unite and to obtain from a monk-loving archimandrite a little stability. That's your opinion, and we endorse it... And about uniting: also, our spiritual father, father Theodore, repeatedly confirmed that we should not be separated, but cohabit together. Especially when before his death he received the gift of foresight he tried to persuade us in a fatherly way like this: 'My fathers! For the sake of the Lord, don't separate from each other, at the present most miserable time you can find but a few with whom you can breathe a word in good conscience.' But you see this with your own experience as in a mirror. Unfortunately, however, because of my many sins there is in our alliance no such courageous and worthy person who could govern a monastery and nourish us according to the tradition of the fathers and edify us cautiously... But to get together seems useful to reinforce each other."

Father Leo's wish became known in the orthodox world. Several monasteries invited him to settle there with his disciples. The archbishop of Kazan Ambrose (Podobedov) was willing to take him in his eparchy. Filaret, the archbishop of Kaluga, the hegumen of Optina Daniel and the founder of the Optina skete Moses invited him, too. In addition, he was invited to the Ploschanskaya hermitage in the Orlov diocese. father Leo refused to move to the Kazan diocese. "Our hearts," he wrote, "are inclined to go there (to the Optina monastery), because I made a start there and lost my health there. And our former supporter and benefactor, his eminence Filaret, a monk-loving soul, desires it so." In 1823, when visiting the Optina monastery, bishop Filaret of Kaluga said the prophetic words: "I feel that father Leo will certainly live in the Optina monastery or at least in this diocese." The prediction of the bishop came true, but after the lapse of more than five years.

Father Leo's increasingly urgent requests to be released from the Alexander-Svirsky monastery remained unanswered. For five years father Leo was not allowed to leave the monastery. They did not even let him go on a pilgrimage to Kiev. As he himself wrote in a letter to father Joannicios: "May you take as an example also the story of my stay in Svirsky. Five years against my will. And although apparently there was no strong oppression like you experienced, those who felt it by experience, saw it... And you yourself suggest that I undergo this great funeral feast organised by the main superior like a martyr... But you and I forget about the long-suffering man in whom the whole church indulges and who uttered those words: "If we accepted good things from the hand of God, why should we not accept bad things?" (Job 2:10)

Of course, for the life of the monastery and visiting people this was a great spiritual benefit. "Hey, there is nothing we feel so sorry about as to leave here the remains of our most kind benefactor, very blissful father Theodore," said father Leo. "However, also about this may the will of our Creator and Redeemer be done! We think and judge like men, and the more so like *carnal* men. But the most merciful Lord knows all, and even the deeds we have not done..."

"Where the will of God is done," he wrote elsewhere, "there are no very strong obstacles to overcome." His faith was justified by the events that followed. At the beginning of the sixth year the Lord arranged it so that he was finally discharged. When father Leo left the Alexander-Svirsky Monastery he went on a pilgrimage to Kiev. In the distant caves he listened to the early Liturgy. During the Liturgy a schismatic took the opportunity to steal the hand of the relics of the venerable Benjamin. The search started. The cave-dwelling monks turned to father Leo with the question whether he had any suspect in mind. Father Leo described the distinguishing features of someone who in his opinion was a suspect and mentioned the exact moment when he went out of the cave. Using the description of father Leo, the monks found that person which indeed turned out to be the thief. The sacred object was recovered.

When father Leo came back from Kiev, he did not set out for the Optina monastery, but he went first to the Ploschanskaya monastery of the Mother of God in the Orlov eparchy. This happened on October 6th, 1828. In the Ploschanskaya monastery father Leo met hieromonk Makarios, a monk engaged in ascetic exercises. This meeting was not an accident but the providence of God. In father Leo Makarios found exactly what his soul had so long yearned for: a man with spiritual discernment, which according to Isaac the Syrian the fruit of resisting temptations. Manly relying on God in temptations had helped father Leo to become an exceptional expert in the struggle against visible and invisible enemies. Therefore, he could be of help to those who are tempted. (Heb. 2:18) Father Makarios passionately loved his holy monastery. It was his custom to praise it and he advised many who wanted to enter a monastery to stay there. But father Leo, to whom by the grace of God the future of the Ploschanskaya monastery was revealed, always used to say to father Makarios: "Wait a little, wait a little! You'll see what Ploschansk will be like. Ouch, you'll be really perplexed." These words of father Leo soon began to come true. According to the unknown ways of God's providence some discord and dissension emerged between the monks so father Leo could stay only six months in the Ploschanskaya monastery. In April 1829 he moved to the Optina monastery.

Chapter 7. Spiritual mentor of the Optina monastery

Father Leo arrived at the Optina monastery already in his declining years. He was of big stature, majestic. He always kept upright despite his unhealthy weight. His step was easy and confident. The soul of father Leo was filled with great love and compassion for his fellowmen. His personality radiated a sensation of fearless power and stately calm. In his presence grief and vain thoughts disappeared. The hearts of people around him opened to God and became filled with a sense of calm, peace, inner joy.Nobody ever saw father Leo sad, angry or short-tempered. The great directness of his mind did not tolerate hypocrisy, sugary words of conventional "piety". Father Leo cannot be judged as an ordinary man because he reached that spiritual height from where the ascetic acts according to the will of God. He was not afraid of human judgment and feared only God's judgment. He left all small precautions aside and leaned on the Lord Jesus Christ and his holy guardian angel. He entrusted himself and his visitors to their invisible leadership. And he always remained steadfast against the attacks of enemies, visible and invisible. That is why his words were courageous, simple, and often sharp. He did not care about refinement or beauty of expression, about softening his words, he told everyone the truth without considering how people will react to it, to everyone he said "you". This applied not only to laity who came to him, but also to the brethren and other spiritual mentors. He spoke to them with extremely clear language and always with a touch of humour. It seemed he was trying to hide his elevated inner states in jokes in order not to discomfort those whom he addressed. In his manner of expression and action he often resorted to somewhat playing a Christ's fool wishing to disguise his spiritual wisdom and insight. Instead of much persuasion he sometimes immediately cut the ground from under somebody's feet and gave him to understand and feel his inconsistency and wrongness, and thus with his spiritual scalpel he would open an abscess in the hardened heart of his collocutor. As a result, that person would shed tears of repentance. Father Leo knew how to achieve his goals. It happened that some of the visitors to the monastery got acquainted with some of the brothers, who were indifferent to father Leo, or opposed him. Thus, many did not come to talk to him. "Hey, do not worry," he said in response to the indignancy of his disciples, "people always find exactly the place where they belong." When someone sincerely and with all his soul seeks salvation, the Lord will lead him to a true mentor. But if someone comes because of self-interest, self-will, disbelief, or self-importance and self-justification, he will miss the opportunity to contact a true mentor. Father Leo called all sentimental manifestations of affection "fanaticism". "I stayed near father Theodore without any fanaticism," he used to say, "while inwardly I wanted to fall to his feet."

But when father Leo, still a novice, left Optina monastery, it was just starting to revive through the prayers and works of father Abraham. What had happened to Optina in those 30 years?

Chapter 8. The history of the skete

A skete was built for a silent and reclusive life. It became the heart of the Optina monastery, the cradle of future spiritual mentors and of inexhaustible gifts of the Holy Spirit to those who labour and have been burdened (Matthew 11:28).

In December 1820 bishop Filaret (Amphiteatrov) of Kaluga addressed himself in a letter to the well-known spiritual mentor hieroschemamonk Athanasius who lived with his disciples in the Roslavlsky woods with a letter:

"Venerable father Athanasius, beloved brother in the Lord! Your brother and my spiritual son schemamonk Bassianus proclaimed to me that you have the wish to find for yourself and your likeminded brothers a place at the Optina monastery of the Presentation in the Temple to most conveniently advance on the path of monastic exploits. The same was confirmed by father Moses who visited me when passing through Moscow. If such is your desire, I am ready to receive you and the other monastery-dwellers who you believe it is right to take with you. I'll receive you with love and I would consider it a special grace of God to my unworthiness. I will let you choose a place for yourselves at the monastery hermitages. You can choose any place you like for a silent and eremitic life and follow the example of the holy monastery fathers. The cells will be prepared for you, as soon as you have expressed your consent. You'll be totally free of monastic obedience's. I assure you with my pastoral word that I will use all my influence to ensure you are given peace. From my youth I've loved the monastic life with all my heart; I will find true joy in spiritual conversations with you.

I call the blessing of God upon you and pray the Lord Jesus Christ that He will fulfil your good wish, with my true respect to you and brotherly love I am the zealous servant of your reverence, pilgrim Filaret, bishop of Kaluga.

1820, the 15th day of December. Optina monastery.
P.S. Also the current father superior, hegumen Daniel will be glad about your coming. He is a very good man, wise and peace loving. You'll come to love him."
Father Athanasius replied to the bishop:
"Your eminence, gracious father!
I, the most low and unworthy person, was touched to have been favoured to receive from your eminence a writing full of archpastoral gentleness and love especially for the monastic rank. Because of my cowardice and unworthiness, I did not have the courage to approach your consecrated person with an answer: but looking at the great benevolence of your eminence to all I dared to write about myself. From the letter of your eminence, I see you have the well-intentioned wish to establish at the Optina monastery of the Presentation in the Temple a skete for those inclined to an eremitic, silent life following the example of the ancient holy monastery fathers. On this standing you are favourably disposed to invite me, the most unworthy person, and other monastery-dwellers of my group who are appropriate for this. I, a feebleminded one, know the benefit of silence in a small and unanimous group from the testimonies of holy men and to a small extent from my own former novitiate. Therefore, I am inclined to surrender to your archpastoral will with soulful joy. But herewith I dare to explain to your eminence, that when God favours us to lay a foundation for establishing a skete and to bring it to perfection, then it is desirable that this foundation of monastic life could be formalised and inalterable. The skete should not cause the dissatisfaction of the monastery in any way. In particular, the skete should not waver away from the monastery. Both habitations should mutually support each other, and a spiritual union of love should be observed. There should be no question of envy between the institutions under your God-wise episcopal patronage.
From our side we hope to be loyal to the overall peacefulness by the following two principal means:

First, if possible the skete should have separate means of support with the help of which the God-loving souls will be able to get along themselves without having to plague the monastery with needs, so that they can somehow plant vegetables in the garden, and so that at times who is able to may engage in needlework if he is in low spirits. Nevertheless, we chiefly rely on God's providence, that He would not deprive us of the necessary supply of provisions. When there will be an excess of something we will give it to the monastery, and when there will be a deficit we will be as enduring as possible.

Secondly, it is necessary for the general silence to prevent worldly people who are motivated by curiosity to enter the skete, otherwise silence cannot be kept; The brothers of the monastery should come to the skete only on Saturday or Sunday and only with the blessing of the father superior. The other five days the skete should be left by everybody in perfect silence.

On such foundation, but even more so on your archpastoral authority, we rely as to make the most of the eremitic life. When our fellow brother and spiritual mentor father Moses resolutely proceeds and his current brothers with him, then with love also I will follow them. I only have to confess to your eminence about my feebleness: I cannot combine the position of hieromonk and superior and agree to be on a par with the monastics.

Nevertheless, I throw myself at your archpastoral feet. In complete devotion I beg your archpastoral blessings and prayers. I place my trust in them.

Your Grace! Gracious father and archbishop, your lowest servant of all, unworthy schemamonk Athanasius"

1st April 1821.

To this message of father Athanasius there was the following response:

"Venerable father, schemamonk Athanasius, dear brother in the Lord!

I was sincerely gladdened that the Lord Jesus Christ put in your heart the good idea to settle with the brethren in Optina monastery. At your request I entrusted father hegumen Daniel to allot space in the monastery's bee-garden. It should be a decent space and quite convenient for life in skete. He will authorize the zealous benefactor merchant Briuzgin to build cells.

When you arrive here with the brethren then establish in a formal way also the rules for skete life according to your ideas and in the spirit of the holy monastery fathers. Your silence will be protected, both from the side of the monastic brethren, and from worldly people.

On receiving the news of your arrival I'll hasten to see to it for you to be able to mutually advice each other on how to take care of this holy and godly matter.

I call on you and your God-pleasing brethren the blessing of God. I remain, always with sincere love for you.

Your reverence's most zealous servant and brother Filaret, bishop of Kaluga.

I ask you to testify to father Moses of my love. I am very grateful for his writing to me. I will not write him especially, because I am sure that you are one at heart.

24 April 1821"

On the 6th of June 1821 the hermits came to the Optina monastery from the Roslavlsky forests led by monk Moses (Putilov) and they settled in the monastery's bee garden.

The original skete brotherhood consisted of six people: father Moses (Putilov), who became head of the monastery, his brother father Anthony (Putilov), father Sabbatios, novice John (Drankin), as well as schemamonk Bassianus and monk Hilarion, who had joined the Roslavlsky monks already in Optina. Filaret approved a plan of buildings for the skete drawn up by father Moses, and there started in Optina a new monastic life...

Soon the construction of the skete church in the name of John the Forerunner began. The bishop donated the iconostasis. The church was consecrated in early 1822.

Father Moses then turned to the bishop for permission to receive the schema. "The time has not yet come," said Filaret and made another proposition: to accept a clerical order. Moses did not want to become a priest and decisively refused. Then Filaret said: "If you do not agree, I will bring charges against you at the Last Judgment." The threat had its effect: the hermit agreed and was ordained a hierodeacon, and on 22nd of December 1822 he became a hieromonk. Then he was appointed treasurer and confessor of Optina.

He continued to organize the skete. He erected new buildings that required large expenditures. In 1825, when he was 43 years old, he was appointed father superior of the skete. And for 47 years he remained its father superior. The number of brethren doubled in that time. The possessions of the monastery increased. Large herds of cows, orchards and various workshops multiplied the wealth of Optina. They built two churches, a refectory, seven quarters with cells, guesthouses, cattle yards, stables, and an outer wall which was whitewashed. Father Moses always started big undertakings without having the means for it. He relied on the help of God alone. With each new venture practical people would ask: "What about the money, father Moses, do you have money?" With a smile the father superior would show 15-20 roubles. "But this is like nothing, because it is a construction of many thousands." Father Moses would reply: "But you forgot about God. I do not have money, but He does." To pay the workers often there were left only some copper coins. Then father Moses would ask to wait a bit, and in a day or so the required amount would be delivered by mail. When the money did not come, he would not hesitate to take a loan, but he returned his debts without delay, as soon as possible. It can be said that the economic activity of father Moses was entirely based on the Gospel: "do not be anxious about tomorrow ..." (Matthew 6:34) Never save money, always allow it to roll so that it does not remain in one place; to return earthly treasures to God through the hands of beggars.

Sometimes he undertook great works only to come to the aid of the needs of the local population. During a famine, when also in the monastery there was a lack of bread, father Moses hired local peasants for a new building. The possibilities however did not run out: the father superior bought bread at a very high price and fed the people. Some of the people around him dared to reproach him for these too great expenses. Normally father Moses was reserved and taciturn, but he answered with indignation and with tears in his eyes: "Oh, brother, you think we are of the likeness of an angel? What did Christ our Saviour voluntarily accept death and sacrifice His soul for? Why then did He preach words of love to us? In order for us to repeat His great words about loving our neighbours in vain and just with our mouths? ... Well, should the village folk die of hunger? But they ask in the name of Christ to be saved from death by starvation, and Christ is love. No, we will take action for the very village folk themselves while the Lord has not yet closed His generous hand for us. He does not send us His gifts for us to hide them under a bushel, but for us to return in such a difficult time to the same people from whom we received them."

Father Moses was always ready to help those in need. Once the cellarer wanted to sack the stove builder who had cheated him more than once. The stove builder, a poor peasant, begged for forgiveness and promised to improve. "He will never correct, father," said the cellarer. "He is a well-known villain." The father superior got angry: "What, the man wants to improve, and you say that he is a villain? You're a villain yourself!"

In the monastery there was guest house which housed pilgrims and visitors, each paid as much as he liked. One could put money in a special can. One wealthy merchant told father Moses that in that way he receives a great number of people in the monastery who do not pay for their stay in the monastery. "If ninety nine do not pay, God will send the hundredth who will compensate for all," answered the father superior. 'Well, this hundredth must be me then,' said the merchant and donated a substantial amount of money to the monastery. Father Moses would not be surprised with any, even the most sizeable offering.

One day a family came to the monastery that had done many good deeds to the monastery and that had made many donations to it. They settled in the guest house, but they were dissatisfied with some arrangement of the guest house administrator. They came to complain to father Moses: "Look, father, we always diligently receive your collectors, we try to make them at ease in all kinds of ways, with love we help the monastery as much as we can, but your administrator did not want to do so-and-so for us." "But we thought," answered father Moses, "that you did your benefactions to us for the sake of God and that you expect rewards for your good deeds from the Lord. If you expect rewards from us, sinners, then it is better not to do benefactions for us because we, wretched and useless sinners, can give nothing in return." The visitors were satisfied, and they were comforted by the sincerity of father Moses. Afterwards they themselves remembered with delight and gratitude how they had expected apologies and instead of their self-love being satisfied they had received highly spiritual edification. Later of course father Moses sent for the administrator and made him listen to reason.

In his external activities father Moses was able to find principles of "Christian domestic administration" and put them in practice. Like no other, he was able to "attract money" and at the same time he wanted Christian poverty more than anything in the world. "Rich poverty", as father Moses used to say. He never demanded deposits from novices when they first came to the monastery. He loved to take in crippled, blind and good-for-nothing people into his monastery, although they could not be of any use to the monastery. He never made people feel his power, but he ruled the life of the monastery with a firm hand. Being by nature a man given to anger, he made efforts to accumulate great gentleness in his contacts with the brothers. When he would feel his anger starting to seize him he secluded himself immediately in his cell. And he would not leave it until he had found inner peace in prayer. Nothing escaped the eyes of father Moses, but as a rule, he refrained from immediate action when it was necessary to reprimand one of his monks. He would allow some time to pass and then he just reminded the brother of the mistake he had made. Prior to making a remark to anyone of them, the father superior would pray a long time for him, and he would make sure that the brother was in the spiritual state necessary to effectively perceive his admonition. He had boundless confidence in the good will of man and he often repeated the words of John Chrysostom: "One should only doubt about the improvement of those who are in hell with the demons." He avoided strict measures as regards the brethren and said that you should always wait for the Lord Himself to touch the heart of a person. From the diary of father Moses: "1819, December 15th. During the meal, an understanding gleamed in my mind regarding the brothers I am living with. Whatever their errors, whether I saw them, or they confessed them to me, I should take them upon myself and repent for them as if they were my own, so as not to judge them severely and not to blaze up in anger... Let the mistakes, misdemeanours and sins of my brothers be mine."

That's how under father Moses the Optina monastery was transformed from an impoverished coenobitic monastery into one of the most popular Russian monasteries. And not because of there being there some great object of worship as for example in the Trinity Lavra of saint Sergius or the Kiev Lavra. But solely by virtue of its spiritual harmony.

Unlike other monasteries where inhabitants were people of one class, mostly from the common people, the monks of Optina were from different social classes. There were educated people as well as nobles, and clerics, and peasants. Even among the educated class which used to shun monks Optina enjoyed fame and respect. This was due to the fact that father Moses accepted into the monastery all the aspirants according to the word of the Saviour: "...him that cometh to Me I will in no wise cast out." (Jn. 6:37) Each of them brought into the life of the monastery something of his own: common people - their pure and childlike faith, unpretentiousness, and humility; educated people - their enlightened view of monastic inner work expressed in a more subtle and profound understanding of Scripture and of the writings of the holy fathers. The father superior and the spiritual mentors united the brothers in one close family. With their wise counsel they smoothed out the shortcomings and vices of individual monks. They reconciled quarrels, they did their utmost to implant in the brotherhood love of one another, they showed by their example a loving, warm-hearted attitude to the needs of their neighbour. This created the spirit of Optina which attracted so many people. There was neither the usual cadging nor the hypocritical servility that can quickly turn into impertinence. The monks did not take pains to imitate secular, gallant people as in the Lavras nor did they, on the contrary, try to make a show of their ignorance and rudeness, which belong to a popular misconception of true asceticism. Thanks to the enlightened hegumens and the spiritual mentors there was among the brethren not that hatred and animosity against the educated person which sadly characterize even the most well-known Russian monasteries. You could not hear phrases there of such kind: "We do not really need these scholars, give us a worker who could bake bread or knows a craft, because the scholars are incapable of any hard work." No! They were very well aware there that while for manual labour the commoners and unskilled labourers are necessary, in order to preserve a high level of the monastic spirit educated people were needed. Just give them suitable work, and then they will turn out useful members of the monastery's community, and not a kind of spongers and chairwarmers.

As he himself had passed through the school of asceticism and was familiar with the statutes of the ancient monastic cloisters, father Moses knew clearly that neither by wealth, nor by beautiful singing of the church choir, nor by adorning the church and such the spirit of a brotherhood can be elevated. It can be elevated only through spiritual guidance of the God-enlightened mentors. That is why his first and foremost concern was the establishment of spiritual mentorship in his monastery.

Spiritual mentors are granted by God a mysterious blessing by which the whole depth of the human being is revealed to their spiritual eyes. With their spiritual sight they see all the hidden sides of the soul, all that is hidden in the mind, and all that remains hidden to the consciousness of people. Generally, a person is not aware of his own depth. "Our fancied though non-existent qualities hinder us to struggle against our invisible but very real sins," said Filaret of Moscow. "Often, we create a false impression about ourselves, we make of ourselves some artificial and conventional 'self', which serves us as a kind of 'key' to all external relations, and this mask often becomes a disguise that substitutes even for ourselves, our true identity as it stands before God."

In such a condition - blinded, shackled by sins – the unrepentant conscience is unable to break free, to stand up straight at the sacrament of penance; Christians do not know how to confess, and confessors often cannot help them.

It is not enough to receive the absolution for committed sins, we must straighten our conscience, regain freedom too. Too often confession becomes mechanical. The priest addresses himself to an unreal, generalized sinner, because he - the priest - often only knows sins abstractly and impersonally. But a spiritual mentor is always facing a human individual with its unique inimitable destiny, with its confession and its own difficulties. Due to a special gift of God he sees each person as God sees him and he tries to help him by revealing to him the inner meaning without violating his will in order for the human individuality to come to light free from hidden shackles.

Even a deep knowledge of human nature, which is acquired through long experience is not enough to help a person spiritually. It is necessary to have an insight in person's depth, which God only can reveal to the one who wants to help. The principal difference between a confessor and a spiritual mentor is that a confessor prompts people to embark on the path of salvation while a spiritual mentor guides people on that path.

Chapter 9. Working days in the skete

In 1829, at the time of the arrival of father Leo at Optina, the construction and arranging of the skete had not yet been completed. Everything was shabby. There was a simple, small wooden church in the middle of the skete in the name of the Holy Prophet and Forerunner of the Lord John, with a modest iconostasis. Next to the wooden church there was a bell tower with small bells. Around the church there were a few small wooden houses with their roofs covered with planks. The territory of the monastery was partially enclosed with a wattle fence. A dense forest with huge fir and pine trees and with thick greenery surrounded it on all sides. On the north side of the skete there was a marked place for the bee-gardens and there stood the small house of father Leo too. The place for his little house, a little to the side of the skete, was not chosen by chance. According to the statutes of the skete, women were forbidden to visit the skete, and the entry of men was restricted. Father Leo did not make a difference between male and female, aged or young and in each he saw only a person who should be comforted in affliction and directed to the path of salvation. Therefore, in order for everyone, both men and women, who wished it, to be able to freely visit father Leo, and in order for the silence of skete life not be broken, it was built slightly to the side. Part of his disciples remained with father Leo to assist in moving and to start arranging domestic life, while others settled in the skete.

Father Moses placed himself under the spiritual leadership of father Leo, and he committed the whole brotherhood to his spiritual nourishment.

The way of life in the skete was austere. Here is how Ignatius (Brianchaninov) describes it, at that time he was a novice and a disciple of father Leo: "All skete dwellers then constituted a spiritual family. Peace and love reigned in it. All were characterised by deep humility. Each tried to outdo the other in this regard. We were even afraid to offend each other with a glance and asked for forgiveness at the slightest insult to a brother. All observed silence.

We did not go about the cells to visit each other. Some only came out occasionally for solitary walks in the skete at nighttime. Beginners were instructed not so much with words as by the example of life of the experienced monks. A good example of the elder brethren had a beneficial effect on them, disposing them to emulate them. It was obligatory for all to appear for general obedience (except for certain men of respectable age). In the woods we collected firewood to stoke the cells ourselves. We drank tea only on Saturdays, Sundays and holidays, for which we gathered at father Leo's in the bee-garden. In the cells the brothers did not have samovars. Cooking in the cells and generally keeping provisions in the cells was prohibited. There was not even a trace of vodka or tobacco. For the revelation of their thoughts all the brethren went to father Leo at the bee-garden every day after the evening meal and they also listened to the evening prayers in his cell. Most of all father Leo taught humility."

The life of father Leo was filled with prayer and care for the brethren and visitors. At two o'clock A.M. began the morning rule, then the early liturgy was performed. The evening rule usually consisted of the ninth hour, a selection of twelve psalms, three canons - to the Saviour, the Mother of God and the guardian angel - and the akathist prescribed for that day. Father Leo listened to this rule in his cell. After the evening meal in the skete, we read the compline, the evening prayers, two chapters of the apostles and one of the Gospels. Father Leo always listened attentively to the reading, he made remarks and corrected mistakes; under his guidance fine readers were educated. At that time of the evening, before going to sleep, the skete monks gathered in the father Leo's cell for edification, confession, explanations of the questions and misunderstandings that had arisen. After the reading of the Holy Scriptures - and father Leo often read the Gospel himself - he explained the meaning of what had been read. The father's cell was always full of visitors. Some of the brethren that had come from heavy obediences sat on the floor, but all listened reverentially to the words of the spiritual mentor.

Father Leo particularly revered venerable Alexander Svirsky in whose monastery he had lived for 12 years. In his cell there was a large icon of this saint. He was depicted full-length on the canvas. There also was a large image of the guardian angel and the Vladimir Icon of the Mother of God, a blessing of schemamonk Theodore which father Leo was fond of.

All the time that he didn't pray or worship father Leo devoted to serving others. He ate twice a day simple food. Sleep, including a brief after-lunch rest, took up no more than three hours a day. According to memoirs he said the Jesus prayer or quietly sang church hymns when on rare occasions no people were nearby. Whatever crowds of people he was surrounded with, the mind and heart of the spiritual mentor were never away from God. It is also remembered that during the reception of visitors he had the habit to take up uncomplicated crafts: he would weave belts which he later gave away as a blessing.

Tea drinking with father Leo was remarkable, all the brethren gathered there. The monks were very fond of those moments and took the opportunity to talk in an unconstrained setting with the father. There lived in the skete a certain father Diomede who was advanced in years. He led a strict monastic life and had the desire to teach people, but he had neither the skill nor the gift of spiritual guidance. Therefore, when he communicated with visitors, he made big blunders. For example, there came to him once a lay heavily burdened with sins. He told father Diomede about those sins and asked advice on how to correct his life. Father Diomede, however after hearing the confession began to speak to him, in this kind of tone, with an expression of great terror on his face: "Oh! But how did you dare to do this and that?! Does salvation mean nothing to you?! You will go to hell to be eternally tormented, and you will never be released from there!" Naturally the man was extremely embarrassed and left father Diomede's cell crying from despair and even more heavy loaded than before. But then one of the monks saw this lost, desperate person and told him to ask father Leo's help. After finding out what had happened father Leo admonished him that he should not give up hope and that the Lord descended to earth not for the righteous, but to call sinners to repentance, that His mercy has no limits, and some specific advice on how to struggle with his passions. The man cheered up, regained his good spirits and left. However, father Diomedes continued frustrating his visitors. Father Leo decided to teach him a lesson. An opportunity presented itself when on one of the great feasts, all the brethren gathered in the cell of father Leo to drink tea. However, father Diomede had not come, and father Leo sent a monk to summon him. The messenger returned and said that father Diomede declined to come because he was indisposed. Father Leo knew that father Diomede did not come just because he was unwilling as he did not have the habit of taking tea. He wanted to impel him to submission and obedience, and at the same time to punish him for his aforementioned foolish actions. So, he sent two monks to father Diomede with the following instruction: "Go to him again and carry him in your arms, if he won't walk. And while you carry him throw him in a snowdrift." Two monks went and asked in the name of father Leo: "Please, father, if you are weak, we will carry you in our arms." Father Diomede did not suspect danger and agreed: "Well, carry me if you please." They took the old monk in their arms and carried him, but they chose the largest snowdrift and threw him on it. The little old man floundered a while in the snow, but then he somehow got out and on his own feet and he ran to father Leo with the complaint that his messengers had offended him. Father Diomede was given tea to drink, and he was accompanied back to his cell. Strangely enough since then there were no more complaints by his visitors of the excessive strictness of his spiritual advice.

In conversations father Leo combined reverence and concentration with the simplicity and freedom that were his distinctive traits. His language was easy and at the same time bright and picturesque, full of folk proverbs and sayings, so it was very lively and understandable. He could not stand, as he put it in one of his letters, "the politics of the educated style and the artistic form of address of emotional people." He used to say to his disciples: "Lads! Sell for as much as you bought for." With that he urged to always keep a simple, open form of address, in which there was nothing artificial. "If you were simple-hearted like the apostles," he said one day to a close disciple, "if you did not hide your human flaws, did not pretend to be extraordinarily reverent, were not hypocritical then this path would be the shortest to salvation and it would attract the grace of God. Unpretentiousness, trustworthiness, frankness of the soul, that's what pleases the Lord who is meek at heart: '...Except ye... become as little children, ye shall not enter into the kingdom of heaven.' (Mt. 18:3)" That's why deceitful and hypocritical people could not be pupils of father Leo. He did not like it when someone showcased humility, zeal or reverence and called this a "chimera", that's what folk calls a barren flower on a cucumber plant. "You want to catch my words on the fly," he said to one of his spiritual children, "you want to save your soul *en passant*, you want to learn quickly. This is where your hog-wild enthusiasm, kissing the shoulder or hand of your spiritual father and such-like come from. However, I, being with father Theodore, communicated with him without any fanaticism (father Leo often used this word), while inwardly I wanted just to bow down to his feet with filial respect."

Father Leo could be sharp, and he was not afraid to wound the self-love of his spiritual children if necessary. The way he treated them was always aimed at the eradication of that hidden, deadly vice. He knew well how and to put to cause a blush and bring to reason the one who needed it; but at the same time, he understood precisely the measure of the load one could bear, and how to console and calm. With apparent simplicity, and sometimes even rudeness, his dealing with people was the exact opposite of what we see among people to whom the words of psalm are applicable: "his words are smoother than oil, and they are arrows."(Ps.55:22) Father Leo, on the contrary, expressed, in sometimes harsh forms, the holy truth and a gentle and loving soul and fatherly concern for the salvation of his spiritual children. But there was never rudeness or irritation in this, and it was done solely for the sake of spiritual benefit. "Sometimes," a disciple of father Leo said, "the father made me such a severe and menacing reprimand that I could hardly remain on my feet; but then and there he himself humbled himself like a child, and soothed and comforted me so, that in my soul I felt easy and glad; and I went away from him peacefully and cheerfully, as if the father had praised me, and not rebuked me."

Often, he diluted his edifications and suggestions with a joke. Father Anthony (Medvedev), the future father superior of the Trinity Lavra of saint Sergius, recalled how during his stay in Optina as a novice father Leo dealt with him. "And it happened that I quarrelled with another monk, and my conscience still prompted me to explain my conduct to father Leo. I went to him and began to explain my conduct, that is, trying to justify myself, and to blame the other monk. Father Leo listened, sometimes nodding approvingly to my words. Then, already without hesitation, I started to justify myself more freely. 'Very well then,' said the spiritual mentor at last, 'so you are right, and the other is to blame, that means we're quits; you're righteous now, and you are done with me; why don't you leave since you are saved now. Leave me, because I must use my energy and time for sinners. So why don't you vade in pace together with your righteousness, and do not bother us, sinners.' To improve the situation and to regain the favour of the spiritual mentor I started to explain my conduct even more in details, like 'nothing of the kind, father, because you know: it was such-and-such.' 'Wow, you are even more right,' father Leo commented. 'Well, go, go then, because you know, the sinners are waiting behind the doors of my cell, and you bother them.' I left father Leo as if with bound hands and feet and went back to my cell to calm down. But no, staying just one hour in the cell felt like a year. I went back to father Leo again to explain also this seemingly innocent suffering, but by this I got even more mixed up. And he said: "Yes, you are innocent indeed, but now leave please.' This coming and going repeated itself several times more until in my soul the awareness of my own guilt and peace settled instead of blaming my fellow-monk."

According to many accounts, father Leo was never satisfied by just a formal, outward reconciliation between the brethren. He tried to get both sides to genuinely and unfeignedly forgive offences. He constantly urged disciples to maintain mutual love, peace, and concord between themselves. He often repeated the words of Christ: "By this, all shall recognize that you are my disciples: if you will have love for one another." (John,13:35) In one of his letters it says: "Moreover, we have God's commandment to love our neighbours sincerely, but to claim love from them, that is not said anywhere."

Father Leo tried to direct his spiritual children to a struggle against the passions that rooted deep in the soul. He understood that overcoming self-love, self-importance and other vices is much harder work than carrying out outward exploits, which are necessary too, but only as a means. Brother N persistently asked father Leo to give him a blessing for the constant wearing of fetters. Father Leo didn't give his consent for a long time, admonishing the monk that salvation is not to be found in wearing fetters. Brother N however was still persisting. Then father Leo decided to teach him a lesson. He called the skete blacksmith and said to him: "When brother N comes to you and asks you to make fetters for him, give him a mighty box on the ear." After a while, at the next request of brother N, father Leo said, "Well, just try to go to the blacksmith and ask him to make you the fetters." Brother N gladly ran to the smithy and said: "Father Leo has blessed you to make me fetters." The smith was busy at this time, so he hastily spoke: "What kind of fetters do you need?" - and gave N a box on the ear. Brother N became angry at once and answered the blacksmith also with a slap, and then the two immediately went to seek justice from father Leo. Brother N got then an apt reprimand from him: "How can you wear chains if you could not bear even one slap!"

Father Leo considered enduring insults and offences necessary for salvation. He wrote to a spiritual child of his: "Someone who insults us, we must honour as our benefactor: he is nothing other than a tool with which God arranges our salvation. Thus, we will honour those who offend us as benefactors. And when we start to train ourselves in self-reproach... then our hearts, with the help of the Most High, can become soft and gentle in the spiritual sense. The person is turned into a receptacle of grace and spiritual peace. Then the soul will feel such peace which in the state of pride we are not able to feel or, better said, taste. This peace will enlighten the mind of the hermit... Then he can more aptly ward off evil, subdue the heart and dedicate it wholly to what brings salvation. Displeasure will already seem cheerful and agreeable." Father Leo himself had already reached spiritual peace, which not any sorrow or trouble could disturb. No one ever saw the saint indignant, passionately angry or irritated. In the heaviest days of his life not a word of impatience or grumbling was heard from him, no one ever saw him dismayed.

Salvation of the soul is achieved with much effort only, father Leo often repeated his own saying: "Saving one's soul isn't kind of weaving one's bast shoe[7]." One of the disciples asked him: "Father, how did you acquire such spiritual gifts which we see in you?" The venerable father

---

7 To weave bast shoes: talk bunkum; talk through one's hat; make a muck of something. (tr.)

replied, "Keep it simple, and God will not forsake you and He will manifest His mercy."

Indeed, a novice in the monastery is a product of the world, that is, a proud, vain, voluptuary, money-loving, down-to-earth person. His heart is the sea which 'is great and its hands are spacious. There are creeping things without number.' (Ps.103:25) Or it is a field, all overgrown with thorns. It is necessary to rid this field of thorns, plant good seeds in the soil and take care that they grow and bear good fruit, of course, with the help of the omnipotent grace of God. How much work, knowledge, and skills are required here in this endeavour, exceeding human capacity!? There was a disciple of father Leo who wondered why he did not happen to see miracles from his mentor, while he often heard about this from other brethren. When he came to the elder with the intention of revealing this thought to him, the elder, giving him a blessing, said: "Won't you consider it a miracle to hew such a stump in such a way that something good and useful will eventually come out of it!" The monk immediately realized that he received the answer to his unspoken question. The name of this monk was Alexander, later hieroschemamonk Anthony, the confessor of the Kiev-Pechersk Lavra, known for his pious life, who died on October 10, 1880. He was from the town of Little Arkhangelsk, by the name of Medvedev.

Chapter 10. Ill-feelings of some laity and Optina monks towards father Leo

It is not in vain that the holy fathers say that whoever does a God-pleasing deed, will certainly be tempted. They say too that temptation either precedes or follows every good deed. The enemy of the human race hates not only the very revelation of thoughts, but even the noise of the words of this revelation; for he knows that through this all his intrigues and deceit are destroyed. Therefore, it is not surprising that for introducing spiritual mentorship into the cloisters, a strong persecution began against the mentor father Leo. Not everyone could correctly understand him and his guidance. According to St. Simeon the New Theologian and other holy fathers the laity, who do not possess spiritual reasoning, cannot correctly understand the inner life of spiritual people, just as the apostle Paul says: 'The spiritual nature of man judges all things, and he himself may be judged by no man.' (1 Cor. 2:15).

On the other hand, the ground for the actions of the invisible enemy was very favourable. There were among the former Optina brethren reverent, kind monks, who didn't know much about the spiritual works. Their main pursuits were personal prayer rule, fasting, obligatory attending of all the church services, work in the monastery's workshops and the like. They had no idea about the inner spiritual work. Therefore, when father Leo and his disciples settled in the monastery and started telling to the monks about the spiritual work and spiritual guidance, about the cleansing of conscience and confession of thoughts, about one's cutting off one's desires and reasoning, about inner work, all this seemed to many to be some kind of new, incomprehensible teaching, which some even called 'a new heresy'.

It was also mentioned above that in dealing with people the elder adhered to jocularity, sometimes resembling 'holy foolishness'. And since he always acted openly, not in the least embarrassed and not caring about what people would say about him, some who had no idea about the spiritual life began to criticise him. Some, for example, were provoked by the fact that a schema-monk, who, according to the monastic rule, should use all his time in secluded prayerful labours, was constantly surrounded by people.

They did not understand that father Leo had abandoned his life of silence not for the sake of any selfish goals or vanity, but solely driven by spiritual love for his suffering and infirm brethren, according to the word of the Saviour: 'No one has a greater love than this: that he lay down his life for his friends.'(John 15:13); and that such is the life of an elder, a spiritual mentor, according to St. John of the Ladder, is the greatest feat. Some were provoked by the simple and playful speech and address of the elder, and others by his corpulence, while this corpulence was due to illness. For the elder in the last years of his life ate very little due to indigestion and throughout his monastic life he ate moderately.

The consequence of this was that the older monastic brethren, for whom, due to their old age, it was difficult to change the opinion to which they had adhered for most part of their lives, clearly rebelled against the innovations of father Leo. They became distrustful and hostile towards him and his disciples. Some of the hieromonks, the so-called 'scholars', the widowed priests, often gathered together in the monastery for a group conversation. During one of these meetings a question was raised about a fragment from the Apocalypse. One of the interlocutors, father N., volunteered to puzzle father Leo with this question. Everyone approved of it. Immediately father N. went to father Leo. Father Leo was resting at the moment and kindly invited the visitor to take a seat.

"No, no," said father N, "after all, I came to you for an important matter. What does this fragment of in the Apocalypse mean? Tell me please!"

"Oh, father," father Leo replied, "I don't rack my brains over such wisdom.'

"So, I'll explain it to you," continued father N.

'Well, now, father, have a seat now. It's a big work; but what would you like to have? Would you like a cup of tea?

"Yes, tea, please.

Soon a kind of high tea was served. When father N. had had tea and sweets to his heart's content he said: "Well, let me now explain to you about the Apocalypse."

Father Leo replied: "Where does your audacity, when your belly is just filled to the brim, come to interpret and explain the lofty apocalyptic tales, which the great apostle St. John the Theologian, the confidant and friend of Christ witnessed?" Father N. felt very ashamed and made a hasty retreat.

However, such skilfully arranged lessons of father Leo not only did not soften his foes, but hardened them even more. They began to send reports against father Leo to the diocese. The main accusation against father Leo was that he, being a new-comer in the monastery, was vouchsafed by the father-superior with the task of spiritual guidance of all the brethren. Father-superior was even so much under the influence of father Leo that he didn't undertake any important step in monastery matters without consulting father Leo. The pride of the sour monks was wounded. Their reports did have a consequence. The Kaluga Ecclesiastical Consistory sent a decree to the monastery that all the decisions with regard to any kind of important monastery matters should be taken by the father superior only after consent of the treasurer and four hieromonks from the elder brethren. This was in 1830, only a year after father Leo settled in the Optina Monastery.

However, the expectations of the older monks were not fully realized. The then Kaluga bishop Gabriel (Gorodki) looked at the matter with new eyes. When visiting Optina

Monastery, in the presence of the entire brotherhood, he gave hegumen Moses gracious attention, but he rebuked those who were dissatisfied and ordered them to improve themselves.

Although even after this the protests in the monastery did not completely subside, hegumen Moses and father Leo, who had developed patience because of many years of ordeals, overcame unfavourable circumstances, supporting themselves with the good hope that with the help of God, the monastery would become peaceful again. Their hope in the all-good Providence of God did not deceive them. In time, the anxiety in the monastery subsided indeed.

However soon a new ordeal came for the elder, and now from the side of laity. The invisible enemy of the human race tries to catch everywhere the piously living servants of God. Here is the story of the Kiev-Pecherskaya Lavra's confessor, priest-schemamonk Anthony, who at that time was still a young layman Alexander.

"In December, around the 15th, when I was so eager to see father Leo, I found his disciples in great grief. For their teacher and mentor was at that time summoned by the diocesan bishop Nikanorus to Kaluga, as a result of a report from the head of the gendarmes of Orel, Zhemchuzhnikov by name. He reported that father Leo, on his way to Voronezh and back through Orel met in Orel women, obviously very well-wishing towards him. They all, simple women as well as aristocratic ladies, when meeting him publicly knelt before him in front of everyone and bowed at his feet. Zhemchuzhnikov became suspicious of this. He reported to the Kaluga bishop that he noticed an unusual phenomenon: a simple hieromonk was given a god-like honour, which might indicate one or another sect. The rest of this I've heard from father Leo who told me the following: "I appeared before the bishop, received his blessing and introduced myself.

- Wait, father Leo, - said bishop, - I will now get one job over and then I will get to you.

Having finished the case, he read aloud Zhemchuzhnikov's report to me and asked:

"What do you say to that, father Leo?

I answered: "It is correct, but what am I to do with stupid women? They bow to me as to an idol. However, have no doubts, I do not belong to either a sect or a schism, but am a purely Orthodox son of the Church."

"Tell me then how you believe."

"With pleasure, Your Eminence, but how do you bless me to explain, simply or à la Kiev?

Being surprised by my question, bishop said: "Well, be it à la Kiev."

Having gently cleared my throat I began to say aloud the Symbol of the Orthodox Faith from a very low note, gradually raising my tone with each new part, and took the highest note by "amen," as it is performed in the Kiev-Pecherskaya Lavra at the Divine Liturgy, and concluded:

"So, I believe in and profess the Holy Trinity, and I anathematize anyone who thinks and speaks about It otherwise!"

"Now everything has been proven," said bishop. "I am happy to have the opportunity to work with you.

Taking my hand, he leads me into the study and orders me to make myself at home. He himself took off my hat and cassock, and he himself pointed out all the comforts for the old man. And so, I stayed in the bishop's chambers for more than a week. During this stay bishop became so much in favour of me that, blessing me for the way back, he said goodbye with tears in his eyes."

Father Leo was accompanied on his visit to Kaluga by one of his close disciples, father Paul (Tambovtsev). While father Leo enjoyed the bishop's hospitality, Tambovtsev stayed in a hotel. Every day he would ask about father Leo, and only received the same answer that father Leo was staying in the bishop's chambers. Upon the return of father Leo to the monastery, all his followers were in great joy. Father Leo did not eat anything for two days upon arrival, pleading that he was still full of the bishop's treat.

"On the second day of his arrival,' Fr. Anthony continues his narration, 'I had the good fortune to have an audience with father Leo, being tired of a six-month trip to different monasteries. Then father Leo ordered me to stay in the skete, where I was preparing to receive the Holy Mysteries of Christ and was vouchsafed to become his spiritual son. It felt embarrassed to tell him about what I had heard in the Balaam monastery hotel from two pilgrims from Optina Hermitage about him and the skete and so I didn't. However, on our second meeting, he himself told me everything that was bothering me in the following manner: "Well, what benefit have you gained from your pilgrimage?" So he began.
"Benefit? I responded. "I visited, father, many monasteries and became completely convinced that I would never return to the secular life."
"Where do you like it best?"
"I really liked Balaam."
"I lived there, but here I ended up and got stuck here. But pilgrims and bounders say that I am fat. It's true. Look, what a puffy fellow I am!
I thought to myself: "It's indeed what the pilgrims told me about him."
"But money," father Leo continued, "how can you not love it? With money and with the holy of our time you are getting along nicely. But now, with your pockets empty, you have a bad time. And nothing awaits you at home. This is what bothers your mind all the time now. However, do not be afraid; everything will be fine, just come back soon. You will return to us with an annual permission, so don't worry about it. So how can you not love the rich? After all, they are people too, and some of them are even very much praiseworthy! Oh, brother, you are the last one to reason about these matters. You just look after yourself. Well, you just wanted to tell a lot about yourself, but now you have fallen speechless."
Indeed, I was struck by his swift, half-jocular exposing of what was on my mind, which I fancied was known only to

me and God. For I did not tell anyone about it, and now, suddenly, I see a spectator of the secrets of my soul. What it is? The sweat came suddenly all over my body!

"Don't be afraid, don't be afraid, Sasha-Aleksasha (as father Leo started to call me from that moment, especially in the situations when my faith in him was shaking), don't be afraid, I'm not a magician, neither a healer, nor a deceiver, contrary to what you have heard about me. Get ready to go home on such and such a date. There is a ducky merchant from Belgorod, called Bogatyrev; he stayed with us, simpletons, for half a year, and he got bored. It is exactly with him you will go all the way to your home. You just have been thinking, where to find the means to limp on your way home, while you are exhausted and penniless, and here's a prosperous man, who will moreover be glad to have you as a travel companion."

From the above story, one can clearly see father Leo's unpretentious, joking manner of treating his disciples, and his fatherly love for them on the one hand, and unfavourable rumours about him. He was called a magician, a sorcerer, a quack, and a sect leader. But all this was 'just the beginning of the sorrows' (Matthew 24:8), the 'best' was yet to come.

The spiritual mentorship of father Leo in the Optina monastery lasted from 1829 until the year of his death which followed in 1841, i.e., for twelve years. All this time father Leo suffered almost continuous persecution.

"Schemamonk Bassianus machinated a lot," says the chronicler, "against the superiors, father Moses and father Anthony. He also lived in the skete and abused the confidence in him of the archpastor, who had vested him with the angelic image, that is, the schema... He was jealous that father Moses and father Anthony as well as many secular people revered father Leo, while that they did not pay Bassianus such respect while he fancied that he led a truly holy life..."

Schema monk Bassianus (monk's name Barlaam) was tall and strong, he was stern in his dealing with the brethren.

However, he was respected, as all saw his tireless prayer labours, his austere life. Filaret, the bishop of Kaluga, always visited Barlaam when he was in the skete. Being a man of education Filaret nevertheless loved to talk with Barlaam, who was a semi-literate (he couldn't write, but he could read, the Psalter only, which he knew by heart). A sort of friendship sprang up between them. It was vladyko Filaret tonsured father Barlaam in 1820 into the great schema with the name Bassianus.

Imitating venerable Fr. Seraphim during his seclusion, father Bassianus collected ground elder in the forest. He would dry it and ate it in the wintertime. The monk John, the skete baker, recalled: "It happened I visited father Bassianus, and he treated me to his rotten ground elder. He pulled some leaves out of a pot and offered me saying, 'Well, here you are, oh servant of God, have some meal.' I put it into my mouth, I chewed and chewed, but I could not swallow it and spitted it out. 'You are wrong, oh servant of God,' remarked father Bassianus. Indeed, he ate it without difficulty." Father Bassianus did not have a bed and slept just anywhere, on the floor, on the ground... He was very proud of his schema garments and sometimes he would point at them, saying, "Demons tremble at the schema, they tremble at it, oh servant of God!"

Father Bassianus reckoned himself the co-founder of the skete. Father Moses, Anthony, Sabbatios and he were the long-time residents there. And he was the oldest at that, and even a schema monk. His severe outward ascesis and vanity made him a bitter foe of the spiritual mentorship of father Leo. The settling of father Leo and his disciples in the skete, father Bassianus called 'inflow of evil spirits', and to father Leo and his students he always referred as 'warlocks'.

Father Bassianus especially disliked the fact that a large number of people came to staretz father Leo, and not only monks and nuns, but also the laity of both sexes. He would fall sometimes in an intense frustration and then he complained to the monks of the skete: "I was one of the founders of this skete, but no one cares to know *me*, and look at how many people are there around *him*! It is all witchcraft... I will drive away all this riffraff, those warlocks!" Other ill-wishes of father Leo, who were afraid to oppose him openly, made use of this hatred of the impulsive and naïve father Bassianus, sending slandering reports, full of false accusations against father Leo to the bishop signed on behalf of father Bassianus. He didn't object to this.

Father Leo wrote in 1836: "Let them think about father Bassianus as they please and praise his elevated way of life; but we do not believe him and do not wish anyone to pursue such an 'elevation' of his that bears no fruit. "...by their fruits," it is said, "you will recognize them." (Matthew 7:16) Spiritual fruit is love, joy, peace, patience, faith, gentleness, temperance, abstinence and so on. We feel pity for him and wish him to come to know the truth." Nicholas, the new bishop of Kaluga, supported the monks who were dissatisfied with the works of father Leo as they did not understand the true meaning of spiritual mentorship and had been informing the bishop about him. The situation has become particularly acute in 1835. Bishop Nicholas repeatedly forbade father Leo to receive visitors, and in 1836 he moved father Leo from the skete to the monastery, trying to cut the contacts between father Leo and his disciples. They of course still visited father Leo in the monastery, but it somehow disturbed the established way of life in the monastery and the monastery's brethren were showing irritation with such visits. And the laity eager to find solace in father Leo's admonitions, found their ways too. No prohibitions of hierarchs could make father Leo abandon his duty, that is, to heal the souls of people, to keep them on the path of truth. A year later, the rumour spread that the former founder of the skete, Filaret, metropolitan of Kiev now, would visit the Optina monastery and, of course, the skete. Schema monk father Bassianus was glad to meet again his important friend and thought he would be able to win him over and turn him against father Leo.

The ferry across the river Zhizdra was opposite the village Nizhniye Pryski. Father Bassianus went there. When the metropolitan and the bishop Nicholas of Kaluga who accompanied him left the ferry, he came to the metropolitan and asked for the blessing, as the church hierarchs are greeted. The metropolitan however asked him whether the father superior had allowed father Bassianus to meet metropolitan on his own. Father Bassianus answered in his usual manner: 'No need for his permission, he's much younger than me.' 'Oh, a self-willed one!' Answered the metropolitan. 'You, as a schema monk, should be in your cell and wait for me there. And if I shouldn't come, you must ask the blessing of the father superior to see me.' So, at the very first meeting with the metropolitan father Bassianus failed. The metropolitan and the bishop got in their carriages and drove to the monastery.

Metropolitan Filaret was solemnly received by the brethren, he celebrated liturgy in the church of the monastery, and then passed around all the cells and greeted the Optina inhabitants up to the last novice. In the skete he also visited father Bassianus. "Well, I'm in your cell now," he said. Father Bassianus just began to voice his complaints: "Moses... Leo...," but metropolitan stopped him and said: "Live peacefully and give thanks to God." Saying this he left.

In the chronicles of the skete of 11th of September 1857 the death of father Bassianus is reported. "During his long life he suffered also temptations," it is said there, "but he lapsed in them more out of his simplicity and because of inculcation of malevolent people who stirred up in him envy of the apostolic service of the priest and schema monk father Leo, by misinterpretations of it. Those people incited him to oppose works of father Leo, which he could not grasp because of his simplicity, under the pretext of zeal. However, these are temptations of any man, which happen to anyone on the road of life. All's well that ends well. And his work was crowned with a good, peaceful and painless decease." And further: "The death of this burdened old man was painless, peaceful, and quiet, exactly as is requested in the church prayer. Therefore, we trust that his soul will have a good answer at the Last Judgment by Christ."

During the first six years of father Leo in the Optina skete the persecutions did not have a tough character yet. But over time, the case took a more menacing turn. So, there is a note of a certain Paula Trunova, sister of Paul Trunov, a disciple of father Leo. She tells that one day when she was in Optina father Leo forbade her to come to him the next day, as "there will be a trial." "But who will be judged?" asked Paula. "Well, I of course," answered father Leo. The next day, investigators questioned the entire monastery, but all testimonies were in favour to father Leo. But it was just the beginning. As of 1835, and especially in 1836, the persecutions intensified. Next to many local false reports, the bishop of Kaluga had received an anonymous report, through the Moscow secret police with accusations at the address of father Leo and the father superior Moses. It said that the latter shows unfair preference for the spiritual mentors of the skete, especially father Leo, over the brethren who live in the monastery and that the skete causes great losses to the monastery, and if the skete is not be abolished, the Optina monastery will come to ruin, etc. As a consequence of this report the father superior was summoned for an explanation, and father Leo was not allowed to wear his schema garments (on the grounds that he was ordained privately) and he was strictly forbidden to receive visitors.

"Praised be the most merciful Lord, Who arranges useful things in every possible way... It has become much quieter now in the monastery, and the party of the opponents of quiet disperses little by little. We cherish a hope that it will quieten down even more; I only feel sorry for father S[erafim] who is extremely confused, and rumours reach me that he contrives a lot against me and in his mind he has all kinds of odd ideas about my visits to Belgorod, Borisovka and so on, and he grumbles excessively. Let the

Lord save him and have mercy on him and may the all-merciful Lord grant him to come to his common sense. I feel rather sorry also for A[rkady], the brother of father A., but most of all for the damage against the entire monastic way!" wrote father Leo in his diary.

Venerable father Leo was always seeking only for the glory of God and the good of his neighbour. He used to say: "Even if you'll exile me to Siberia, even if you burn me at the stake, I'll be the same Leo! I do not ask anyone to come to me, but those who come to me by their choice I cannot cast away. Especially among the common people many perish for lack of wisdom, and they need spiritual help. How can I disregard their blatant emotional needs?" Bishop Nicholas had really once again forbidden father Leo to receive visitors and he had threatened to exile him to Siberia if he disobeyed the bishop's interdict. However, father Leo, who was an example of obedience from the first days of his monastic life, in this matter was unbending: following the will of God was to him above all else.

Bishop Nicholas treated father Leo rudely, disregarding his old age. But father Leo endured all oppression that concerned him personally with resignation and placidity, one might even say joyously. The bishop ordered to move father Leo from the skete to the monastery, as part of his intention to reduce the influence of father Leo in the skete. His cell in the monastery was on the first floor and the sick and feeble father Leo had to climb a steep staircase. When his cell-servant grumbled about this inconvenience he said laughing, "What a crank you are, Aleks! Just look how warm my cell is! I'm fully happy. And you say it is inconvenient. Yes, for me, they can put us in the bell tower if they like, if only it is warm."

Another part of bishop's plan of 're-educating' of father Leo was his demand that father Leo attend daily all the church services. The bishop thought that father Leo would have less opportunities to admonish his disciples and the laity. This however had the opposite results. Here's how an eyewitness writes about this: "...it was an odd sight at that time. His way to the monastery church was like a triumphal procession. The people waited impatiently for his appearance. When he came out of his cell many threw themselves on the ground before him, everyone was trying to take his blessing and kiss his hand, some kissed his cassock, and others loudly expressed their compassion for him. It took at least half an hour for father Leo to bridge the short distance between his cell and the church. He walked as if in a corridor between two walls of people. In jest he would fend off with his stick people who crowded up to him to closely. Crowds of people gathered near the right church choir where he usually stood."

Only at the end of the life of father Leo the Kaluga bishop somewhat weakened his oppression. This happened through the intercession of metropolitan Filaret (Amphiteatrov) who loved father Leo sincerely. Nevertheless, during his last meeting with father Leo, the bishop couldn't help expressing his irritation. "Well, old man,' said the bishop, 'you just can't stand away, can you? No matter how earnestly I forbid you, you still keep yourself busy with this muddle-headed crowd. It is time for you to drop it. After all, the hour of your death is drawing still nearer." To this father Leo replied calmly: "Oh holy bishop! Why should I drop something to which I am called. 'I will sing [psalms] to my God, as long as I am.' (Psalm 103:33) And I do try to drive people away from me with my stick, just as you told me, but look, they don't comply. Perhaps you could ask them yourself, directly, why do they come to me? After all, I didn't invite them." But at this proposal of father Leo the bishop burst out laughing and said: "Well, what a ridiculous idea of yours!" However, after this conversation he did leave father Leo alone, thus giving him the opportunity to live and act as he chooses. And the main thing for father Leo was to serve his neighbour, following the will of God: "Go, and act similarly." (Luke 10:37)

Chapter 11. Life and Teaching of Father Leo

In the company of Father Leo people felt spiritual joy, and peace of mind. They often came with sorrows, with grief, and left his cell appeased, joyful. One of his disciples recalls: "I also noticed in myself, while living in a monastery: sometimes melancholy, despondency attacked me, and my thoughts attacked me cruelly. Then I would go to father Leo to find consolation in my sorrows, and when I just entered his cell, the storm of the thoughts/designs disappeared in an instant, and I suddenly felt peace and joy in my heart. Father Leo would ask: "Why did you come?" And I wouldn't even know what to say. He would take some oil from the icon lamp, anoint me, and bless; and I would leave his cell with heartfelt joy and peace of mind."

According to the teaching of St. John of the Ladder, "one's prayer is one's being together and union with God ... the source of virtues and talents." Father Leo was a great man of prayer. While communicating with people around him, he inwardly abided unceasingly with God. The spectacle of great human passions and calamities, of which he was a constant listener, and to which he was compassionate in a sincere, Christian way, drew deep sighs and tears from him, shaking his entire inner. And then he would turn with a sigh to the icon of the Lord or of the Mother of God, in front of which an oil lamp was burning constantly. When there were a few visitors, Father Leo would often immerse so deep in his inner prayer that he did not notice what was happening around him. One of the close disciples of father Leo said that when he was with him alone, father Leo, immersed in prayer, would completely forget about him, did not hear his explanations and made him repeat the same thing several times. Nevertheless, he forbade his disciples not only to take up the elevated mental prayer, but even to speak about it out of fear that they could become of unsound mind.

Father Leo had a living faith in the Divine providence, firm hope and surrendering to the will of God. In all the difficult situations he would gaze with hope to the Source of faith and the Accomplisher Jesus. So, he later wrote (1831) to one of his friends: "Under the impact of a slander our archbishop is displeased with us. But the Archbishop of future blessings, the Lord our God, knows better than this, and consequently can manage us better. And so, I say about this again: let the will of the Lord be done! ... "Remember, the dearest," he wrote another time to his close disciple, "remember our common spiritual father, father Basilios [Kishkin], how he always surrendered himself to the will of the almighty Guardian and Provider. And he did not sin in this, and he reached a safe haven. And he entrusted us to the all-powerful Providence too. He always advised and exhorted us to rely on the Providence of our Redeemer and true Guardian. And the merciful Lord fulfils and turns everything into His will and for our benefit, although apparently by means and actions that feel contrary to us. With the help of the most merciful Lord God, we will endure, and will see... " Even his sorrow for those lost ones subsided due to his faith in God's Providence. "I request you," he wrote to one of his spiritual children, "not to recommend others to visit me. Let them do what they want, but without encouragement. God can help them without intercession of my unworthiness."

The whole life of father Leo was in the service of God and his fellowmen. For the sake of the latter, he was working constantly and exposed himself to great sorrows. He treated his close novices and monks with tender paternal love, calling them "children" and always trying to help them in all their needs. He did not neglect either those of the people whom everyone despised. "One woman, a wanderer," told the priest-monk Anthony Bochkov, "had been constantly near father Leo during his stay in Tikhon's Hermitage and we all got fed up with her. Her fawning on, bows to the ground and various grimaces seemed, especially to me, a comedy and deceit. I dared to tell father Leo that it was not only I, but all our brethren who were annoyed at this stick-at-it one, and that, according to her own words, she was expelled from everywhere, from every monastery, that no spiritual mentor could stand to have her around.

"Are you telling the truth?" Asked father Leo.

"I heard it from her."

"And if I expel her," continued father Leo, "where will she go? And there is a soul in her too, and every human soul conceals a lot of good in its depths. You just have to discover it."

With a sincere disposition towards all his fellowmen, father Leo, however, did not cling to anyone with special exclusive love. Acquaintances and not acquaintances, relatives and not relatives, he paid the same respect to everyone. One day his sister came to him. He received her on a par with other pilgrims and gave her the same gift as he provided to other needy people, that is, he gave her fifteen kopecks. On this occasion, the elder said to some that if a monk would give an extra penny to his relative, then this would show that he had not yet freed himself from the bonds of carnal kinship and did not love all people equally, but differently.

father Leo was fatherly indulgent towards the infirmities of his spiritual children. However, this indulgence of his was combined with holy zeal for piety and prudent severity. Often, he would say: "If you ask me, then listen and act accordingly, and if you don't listen and act accordingly, don't come to me." He wrote to one monk, of whom he was the receiver by the tonsure, when this monk stuck too much to his own mind. "Look! Although I can't tell you directly that you will be excommunicated from our assembly, for the connection of the Holy Gospel is an inviolable union, but by the example of the holy fathers, and especially St. Isaiah of Hermitage, although it is terrible, but to the relief of my conscience, it is appropriate to tell you: Watch out! If you do not listen to your sinful, fake spiritual mentor Leo for the sake of lawful obedience and for the edification of your soul, then your aberration will teach you in a severe way."

During the meal, he had a lively conversation with his students. He allowed modest and gentle jokes and stories that had a spiritual purpose for him. He sometimes told anecdotes from Roman history, which he knew well from ancient translations of Tacitus and other writers. He teasingly called one of his disciples, the aforementioned Fr. Anthony Bochkov, "the last Roman"; perhaps because this disciple used to express an opinion, that their times were the last times of monasticism. Its' decay, according to him, was caused by the same reasons that brought the Roman Empire to its fall: luxury, effeminacy and man-pleasing. Father Leo, however, was like an island impregnable for the worldly spirit, past which the rivers of this world flowed without shaking him in the least. Those who were overwhelmed by worldly confusion were saved from spiritual drowning in his cell, as in a reliable harbour.

Some of the disciples of the elder father Leo, both male and female, told that in the presence of other spiritual mentors, which were strict in appearance and serious in their manner, their souls shrank unwillingly, and they could not freely confess to them their innermost spiritual infirmities. On the contrary, the simple, open, free appeal of father Leo set their souls free, and they easily and freely told him even what sometimes it was difficult for them to admit to themselves. Sometimes father Leo would admonish the guilty in the presence of others, according to the apostolic commandment: "Reprove sinners in the sight of everyone, so that the others may have fear." (1 Tim. 5, 20), not being afraid to upset him or her by this or bring the others in temptation.

People loved father Leo tremendously. Ordinary people had towards him full confidence, they turned to him with all their needs. "I once happened to pass," remembered L.A. Cavelin (at a later date - archimandrite, governor of the Trinity Lavra of saint Sergius), "from Kozelsk to the Smolensk province. On the road in secluded hamlets, when they found out that I came from Kozelsk, villagers hurried to find out anything about father Leo. To the question: "How do you know him?" They said, "Dear goodman, how could we not know father Leo? Yes, he is for us, poor and foolish people, more than our own father. Without him we would be, it seems, downright orphans." There is a monument more eternal than marble and granite!"

His main attention and care father Leo turned to his closest disciples. Not carried away by the desire for an imaginary elevated life and not looking ahead of time for the great gifts of God, he followed the safe path indicated in the writings of the God-wise mentors of monasticism, who teach that the novice ascetic of Christ should first of all be taken care of teaching him- or herself and taming their passions. Along this very path he guided his disciples. Therefore, father Leo especially paid keen attention to the passions soul of those who related to him, and taught everyone to observe those passions, not to act on their suggestion and attraction, but, calling upon God's help, to resist them; above all, do not justify them and acknowledge the disciple's own mental and emotional weakness in them; do not mix vanity, human pleasing or any other impure motives with good undertakings, but sincerely and with pure will, with simplicity and gentleness to serve the Lord.

Once the archpriest John Glagolyev, the diocese supervisor from Belyov, visited the Optina monastery. He and father Leo loved and respected each other. Father Leo was surrounded by peasant women. "What do you find in busying over peasant women," he said with his characteristic plainness. "What of it, father John? And truly: shouldn't it be your business?" answered father Leo. "But then tell me: how do you take their confession? A couple of words, and that's it, the whole confession. But do you enter into their situation, consider their circumstances, sort out what is in their hearts, give them useful advice to comfort their sorrow? Do you do that? Of course, you have no time to bother with them for long. Well, but if also *we* do not receive them, where will they, poor people, go with their grief?" The archpriest was ashamed and acknowledged his words had been too rash.

Father Leo had been given many gifts by the Lord. Before a person would have crossed the threshold of his cell father Leo already knew in what state he was, with what questions and bewilderments he came to him, how he could help or comfort him. One day the rector of the seminary came to the Optina monastery. When it was proposed to call on father Leo, he said: "For what should I talk to him, a peasant?" But when he nevertheless did go to father Leo all the same, father Leo greeted him repeating his own words: "For what should you talk to me, a peasant?" Despite such unceremonious start of the meeting, the rector was not offended, and he talked to father Leo for two hours. Afterward he conveyed his impression like this: "What's our scholarship worth? His scholarship is hard-earned and full of divine grace."

Not seldom it happened that people came to father Leo who were sceptically inclined, they had an attitude of distrust toward him. But their opinion soon changed once they had only personally met father Leo. Not far from the Optina monastery lived a landlord who bragged that as soon as he would have a look at father Leo, he will see right through him. One day this landlord came to father Leo and entered his cell. Father Leo threw a glance at him and said, "What a muttonhead comes in! He came to see right through sinful Leo. But he himself, the scoundrel, has not been to confession and holy Communion for seventeen years." According to the memoirs the landlord was "shaking like a leaf" and then wept and confessed that he was an unbelieving sinner, indeed, for seventeen years he had not confessed and not received the holy Communion.

Father Leo solved all problems, tried to grasp domestic, everyday circumstances. When people found out that matrimonies that he had blessed were always fortunate they started to frequently ask him questions about arranging family life. Father Leo usually advised those who asked him the blessing for matrimony to examine the situation in detail, to make sure that both the bride and groom were healthy and well provided for, and desirably that they were of equal status and age. Poor families he advised not to take a rich bride, so as not to become dependent. He enhanced his advice often by the age-old Russian proverb: "Boots with boots and bast shoes with bast shoes." He told those with questions about the choice of a groom to pay attention to the qualities of his father and concerning the bride - to look at the character of the mother. Finally, he recommended the groom, bride and their parents to listen to their hearts after fervent prayer. If the thought about matrimony brought peace of mind – one could decide to take this step. Otherwise, if there was any doubt, unaccountable fear, anxiety or confusion, it was worth waiting or looking further.

Through the gift of clairvoyance father Leo rescued many from different troubles and misfortunes, because he could warn them in time about an impending danger. Once he kept some merchants who had come to him at the monastery for three days. Later it was found out that during this time robbers had been lying in wait for them. They would have killed them to steal the money that they had with them. There were countless healings through the prayers of father Leo. And not only those who came to father Leo themselves received help, but often he himself took care first. One such a case is well-known. A nun of the convent in Sevsk suffered an incurable breast cancer. Doctors could do nothing to help the patient and stated that she had no longer than three days left to live. During the all-night vigil on the eve of the feast of the Presentation of the Blessed Virgin Mary her suffering became unbearable. Then she got a vision, two old monks come into her cell. One of them said: "Come to me to Optina, pray to God and you will receive healing." The suffering nun gathered her last strength and hurried to go. When she reached the Optina monastery, the two monks immediately came to see her in the guest house, and she recognized them as those from her vision at the feast. The older was father Leo and the younger father Makarios. She had a long talk with them. The next morning father Leo came; he anointed her breast with oil from a lamp and sprinkled it with holy water. Her pain immediately faded away, and in the evening, she was already perfectly healthy. Instead of the three days the doctors had promised, through the intercession of the venerable Leo she lived still more than two decades.

Father Leo also healed mentally ill people; he restored them to new life. One day, three women led a patient, who had lost her mind, to father Leo. They cried and asked him to pray for her. He laid the end of his stole and his hands on the head of the patient and said a prayer; three times he made a cross over her head. The next day the patient was already quite healthy.

Also, many possessed people were brought to father Leo. Amongst them there were those who were not aware of the fact that they were possessed by a demon, and only after father Leo had exposed the charms lurking in them, did they begin to rage. Those were lay ascetics who were engaged in ascetic practices like wearing chains and complained to father Leo that they did not find peace of mind. father Leo explained to them that harsh bodily exploits, without enduring humbly the sorrows allowed by God to come over them, or reproaches from fellowmen, but on the contrary, with grudging in their souls enmity and rancour against offenders, self-conceit, and without the cleansing of the heart from passions, lead to delusion. Father Leo ordered such reckless ascetics to remove the chains, teaching them that excessive bodily exploits without humility and spiritual reasoning, not only do not benefit, but also harm those who are zealous for their salvation, and that Christians should first of all pay attention to the most necessary and obligatory of all the Gospel commandments of the Lord, without observance of which it is impossible to be saved. When, at the will of father Leo, the chains were removed, demons attacked some of those chained by them. Father Leo would place his epitrachelion on such a sufferer and read over them a short prayer from the breviary, and in addition, he anointed him with oil from the lamp or gave it them to drink. As a result of this, there were very many amazing cases of healing. Some then said, and perhaps they will say now: "Yes, it's not difficult; and anyone can anoint with oil and read the prayer. In response to this, one can recall the example of the sons of the Jew Skeva, who began, following the example of the Apostle Paul, to cast out demons in the name of Jesus Christ. "Jesus I know, and Paul I know. But who are you?", answered the demon, (Acts 19:15). The victory over the demons was won by father Leo, of course, after his victory over his passions.

The spiritual activity of father Leo was not limited to the Optina monastery. He often visited the Kaluga Tikhonov monastery where his spiritual son, father Gerontios, was father superior. When father Anthony (Putilov) was appointed hegumen of the Nicholas monastery in Maloyaroslavets many of his disciples also went with him to this monastery. They all would turn to father Leo for advice. Many nuns from convents around were under the spiritual guidance of father Leo. He cared especially for the Trinity Convent in Sevsk, the Tikhvinskaya Convent in Borisov and the Convent of the Exaltation of the Cross in Belyov.

Hegumen Anthony (Bochkov) left us the following description of father Leo: "His face was round, pale and comely because of his spiritual works, with an expression of strictness and courage, framed by a small beard. His hair was thick and long. In old age, it became like a real lion's mane, yellow-grey, wavy, and fell down far below the shoulders. His eyes were small, greyish, they looked straight, his gaze wasn't fixed at the visitor guessing what was concealed in his soul. Because father Leo knew at just one glance what had brought to him one or another stranger, a stranger who could have walked thousands of kilometres. His hands were very slim and beautiful... His height was above average. His gait was beautiful. His manly and at the same time light measured tread showed that he easily carried his quite heavy body. Drooping or stooping of old age was not visible at all in this warrior of Christ who had firmly established himself in spiritual battles." Many remembered that while his form of address was simple, his appearance was truly majestic and inspired reverence and awe at first sight.

Chapter 12. Memories of father Leo by his spiritual children

The story of the novice of Optina Hermitage Alexei Ivanov (Vasiliev)
"Once," he said, "I felt coldness in myself together with subtle embarrassment and reasoned in myself that this was the result of distraction and self-willed action. Three days had already passed since I was not with my spiritual mentor, and did not confess my deeds, and did not reveal my thoughts to him. One thought had been telling me that there was no need to go to him, because during this short time I had done nothing against my conscience. The other thought, on the contrary, urged me to receive from him at least a blessing that could strengthen me against the wiles of the devil. And at the same time, I reasoned in myself that the Lord in His goodness might reveal to the elder about my hidden infirmities, which I do not notice due to my roughness; and if I receive rebuke regarding those infirmities together with his fatherly instruction, then the peace of mind may return to me. Obeying this last thought, I forced myself to go to my mentor. When I entered his room, the elder was busy with guests. Seeing me coming in, he asked: "What do you need?" I went up to him and, kneeling down, said that I had come to ask his blessing and holy prayers. After blessing me, he said, "Thank you." He began to ask how I spend my time; do I do the work of obedience given to me by the superior, that is do I paint the icons entrusted to me? To this I answered: "For your prayers, father, I work." After a pause, father Leo said: "Good; but I heard that you paint portraits too." These words completely confused me, because last evening I painted a portrait of one of my brethren without permission. As a novice, I did not find it necessary asking for a forgiveness properly, and I said that I was "naughty", thinking that I would justify myself. Father Leo, looking

at the guests, repeated this word several times: "He was naughty!" Taking my head and turning my face to the visitors, he said: "Here, gentlemen, this man is over thirty years old and already has a large beard; being a layman, he ruled over thousands of people, he was for some time the manager of the estate of some gentleman. But he came here, to the monastery, to "play pranks". However, he might become useful after all! And sighing, he added: 'Well, brother Alex, so that you will be more accurate in the future, make a few bows. And say during the bowing the following: "Although I am a proud person, I must humble myself. The holy Apostle Paul says: be firm, reprove, and so on." Then, with a cheerful spirit and kindness, he blessed me and said: "Well, my child, now you will be peaceful; vaya con Dios!"

"I once invited a brother to my cell to have cup of tea. While laying the table, I broke a teacup. I went to father Leo to report this and found him sleeping on the bed. He woke up from the rustle and, having seen me, said: "What do you need? Money?" I answered: "I broke a teacup." He immediately called his monk-attendant and told him: "Congratulate Alexis, son of Ivan, he just conquered a city." I didn't understand what the congratulations were for. Father Leo said to me: "Tell me, when will you improve yourself? What good can be expected from you? In the world you were a scoundrel and now you live without improving yourself. If you had the fear of God, then you would have humbled yourself and this would not have happened to you. It can be seen that you've been distracted, not remembering yourself, were engaged in preparing refreshments and because of that broke the cup. And worse still, that in a proud spirit you came to your mentor, boasting: "I broke the cup!". If you were a sensible person, you would come humbly, saying: father, forgive me for God's sake, I accidentally broke a cup; what should happen next? But you speak as if you've conquered a city, you brag. Get out!" When I came to the door, he sighed and graciously said in a gentle tone: "Alexis, son of Ivan! Come back; I hope that you will start working on self-improvement and be more humble in the future." And he ordered the cell attendant to give me a rouble. (All the brethren who were under the guidance of father Leo, if they had any money, did not keep it, but gave it to father Leo, and if anyone needed to buy anything, it was always bought with the blessing and permission of father Leo).

Alexander Smirnov's story

"In the first year of my life in the monastery, I once came, confused to my spiritual father, father Leo, and, crying, told him that when I think about the coming arrival of my mother and sister, I feel embarrassed. Father Leo, thinking that I was overwhelmed by the weakness of earthly love for my mother, and that I regretted abandoning her, got such a zeal for God and annoyance that he hit me hard on the cheek and said: "Do you choose love for your mother over love for God? So, this is how you pay Him for His rescuing you from this world, you weak-hearted?!" Although I wasn't aware of my predilection for my relatives, I rejoiced in spirit, seeing from the act of my father the true spiritual leader on the path to God, Whom he apparently loved above all else, and to Whom, therefore, he also taught me to march without straying.

Then, after some time, I stood once in the inner hallway of father Leo's cell for a long time, waiting to be admitted to him, because of many pilgrims who came to see him from distant places. Having no patience, as an inexperienced novice, I got bored, and finally began to grumble at my spiritual mentor. When his cell-attendant came out from the cell, having left the door of the cell open, I said with annoyance, so that father Leo could hear: "Father Leo feeds strange sheep, while his own sheep hunger." From these words of mine, his cell-attendant became angry and reprimanded me for my impudence and impatience. father Leo, on the contrary, replied meekly and affectionately: "Oh, Sasha, Sasha! Are you confused? Yasha, give him some tea." Then, turning to me again, he continued: "Well, Alexander, have you calmed down? Well, aren't you ashamed to bother about the fact that I receive other people? After all, you want to receive spiritual food from me, but the others want the same, don't they? You are always with me, and others, who annoyed you, came from distant places to see me, to reveal their needs to me and to be comforted, and should I not allow them to come to me? And is it good for us to love ourselves only? On the contrary, God wants us to love others and wish everyone, like He did, to be saved." The truth of his words and meekness softened my heart, and with tears I asked for his forgiveness and felt his gentleness, both on this occasion and during my stay with him.

Comparing this act of his with the first, I began to understand even better about my spiritual mentor; for he did not show a trace of displeasure either in his facial expression or in word for the insult done to him; however for choosing worldly love over love for God, he became angry and could not leave me unpunished for this."

Stories of other Optina monks.

"A novice brother insulted an old monk, and both came to complain to Father Leo. It was obvious to everyone that the novice was all to blame. But father Leo judged in another way. "Aren't you ashamed to lower yourself to the same level as a beginner?' He said sternly to the old monk. "He just came from the world, even his hair has not yet grown back, and it is impossible to charge him if he said something improper. And you have been living so many years in the monastery and have not learned to watch yourself." So, they left. The newcomer triumphed, considering himself completely justified. But soon after this, this brother came alone to father Leo. Father Leo took him by the hand and said, "What are you doing, brother? You just came from the world, your hair hasn't grown back yet, and you're already insulting the old monks!" The unexpected admonition had a strong effect on the brother, and he began to ask for forgiveness. "God will forgive," said father Leo, "just look, brother, correct yourself, otherwise you will be in big trouble."

"At first, after my entering the monastery," said monk N., "I had an excessive zeal for monastic works. Sometimes, after Matins, others go to rest, while I do some work of obedience and then, being tired, I would lie down for a short rest, worrying about not to oversleep, but to be in time for the very beginning of the early liturgy. Someone started waking me up. At the first stroke of the bell, it was as if someone was saying a prayer at my door. I got up and looked, but there was no one there. The next day again. I thought about father I. I went out, but there was no one. I told about all this to father Leo. "What do you think," he asked me, "who is waking you up?" "I think, father," I answered, "it is perhaps an angel?" "An angel with horns," F. Leo objected. "We'll see what happens next." The next day no one woke me up and I overslept for the service. The next day and the third day I overslept yet again. So, both of us were ashamed - and my unknown wake-up caller, and I, a gullible zealot."

"One day, father Leo's spiritual son, who was devoted to him, came to him, after sitting in his cell for the whole evening, and he asked father Leo: "I saw how the brethren came to you and how you received them. One brother came before everyone else, but he kept waiting and came up to you as the last one. Others, having arrived, waited a bit, then approached you and asked what they needed. Some did not want to wait at all, and as soon as they came in, they immediately pushed forward, trying to make you to receive them immediately. What Is the difference between them? father Leo answered: "There is a difference, a big difference. He who having come to me, does not want to wait and pushes himself forward, ahead of everyone, cannot keep in his memory for a long time what I said to him. He asks me yet again and still forgets. And he who, having come to tell me about his needs, patiently and humbly lets others pass before him, will have every word he hears firmly imprinted in his heart, and he will remember for a lifetime what he was once told.""

"In the summer of 1833, a twenty-year-old youth, Paul Trunov, came to Optina with his younger brother Simeon. After they had abandoned their home without saying a word, their parents at first mourned for them, even wept and grieved greatly. However, when they came to know that their children entered the monastery, they forgave them their trespass. Meanwhile, after some time, parental love prompted their father, Theodosius Trunov, to write a letter to his children in Optina, in which he earnestly asked at least one of them to come to see their parents. With the father Leo's blessing, it was decided that Paul would visit them. He immediately set off. Let us note here that Teodotas, as a pious man, loved to read the Life of the Saints by St. Demetrius of Rostov during his leisure hours. Just before the arrival of Paul, he read in the story of St. Nicolas of Myra about a youth, who was taken as a prisoner by the Persians and made a servant in the chambers of their prince. However, owing to the ardent prayers of his parents, this youth was suddenly taken away by an invisible force from captivity and returned to his parents, still in Persian clothes and with a cup in his hand filled with wine, that he was serving to the prince. Theodosius fell to thinking of this legend: "How touching! If something like this would have happened to me, I couldn't bear it."

But suddenly the door opened, and his son Paul, in monastic clothes, entered the room. Theodosius did not recognize him, and asked him, who is he. Having crossed himself in front of the holy icons, Paul bowed to Theodosius at his feet and said: "Dear father, I am your son Paul." Theodosius was stunned, and the book fell out of his hands; he could hardly recover from the joy that he saw before him his son whom, he thought, he would no longer see in this temporary life. After spending some time at his parents' house, Paul returned to Optina monastery.

From the very beginning of entering the monastery, Paul completely devoted himself to the obedience to and the guidance of father Leo, to whom he revealed his deepest thoughts and designs. In relation to the monastic brethren, he was so meek and mild-mannered that not one of them ever heard from him an insulting word, or an insulting argument, or grumbling at anyone or for anything at all. Throughout his stay in the monastery, which turned out to be not long, because of his illness, he fulfilled the monastic obediences with patience.

It happened that some of the brethren murmured at him and insulted him for his not accomplishing work timely, and called him lazy, while this failure was due to his sickness and lack of strength. Paul, like a gentle lamb, either remained silent, or would say something like: "I'm sorry, for God's sake, I'm weak." However, the reproaches of brethren caused his heart pain. Often, with tears in his eyes, he came to his spiritual father and mentor, father Leo, and poured out the grief of his soul before him. Father Leo would speak to him, consoling: "Be patient, Paul! For it is said in Holy Scripture: "it is necessary for us to enter into the kingdom of God through many tribulations." (Acts 14:21). And nowadays it is like this: "Whoever does harm, he might still do harm. And whoever is filthy, he might still be filthy. And whoever is just, he may still be just. And one who is holy, he may still be holy." (Rev. 22:11). So, let us "advance, through patience, to the struggle offered to us." (Heb. 12:1). And the Lord said: "By your patience, you shall possess your souls." (Luke 21:19). And with those and other words from the Holy Scriptures, father Leo pacified Paul's troubled soul, bringing him to inexpressible joy, making clear to him that everything which happens to him is done according to the will of the Lord, to test his zeal. That all sorrowful cases should be accepted as God's inexpressible mercies, and that the disease was given to him from God, so that he may he glorify His holy name. Father Leo thus was teaching Paul the deep introspection, self-reproach.

The sickness that Paul had long felt was the threshold of phthisis. His body gradually melted like a burning candle, but his mind was immersed in an incessant prayer. It is remarkable that he knew the entire Psalter by heart.

Almost a year before his death, he always said: "Ah! I will die soon; pray for me, fathers and brethren." The year 1836 had come. The phthisis in Paul has intensified. Father Leo told his close brethren: "Paul will be taken from us during Holy Week." Throughout the winter, Paul could barely walk, and in the fifth week of Great Lent he no longer got out of bed and only prayed. Often, he called on Father Leo, and then only he was at peace when he talked with him. From that time on, he often confessed. On Lazarus Sunday, he was clothed by the father superior in Schema and received the Communion. On April 2, on Thursday of Bright Week, during Matins, he was specially ordained, and after the liturgy he received the Holy Mysteries of Christ again. After that, Father Leo told him: "Well, Paul, you will get well soon." "I know, father," answered the sufferer, "but not in this life." The evening of Bright Thursday was approaching. The bed of the dying man was surrounded by some of his friends. At seven o'clock in the afternoon he closed his eyes and said something incomprehensible. At this time, father Leo himself said the prayer for the dying, and Paul looked at him first with surprise and then thanked him.

Father Leo asked: "Do you wish me to come to you again?" He replied: "I so wish that you would be with me until the very death." He said this clearly and loudly and from that moment on he changed completely. Then, getting up, he sat until his most blissful death and was fully conscious. Then he asked his cousin Hermogenes, who was with him, to put him on a pillow, but as soon as he moved Paul, he sighed and gave up his spirit. It was at nine o'clock in the evening. The triple chime of the bell announced to the monastery brethren the passing away of Paul's soul. The brethren gathered around the cell of the newly deceased, and Father Leo again himself performed the "Prayer on the Departure of the Soul from the Body" over him. The face and whole body of the dead man turned white and was soft, like a living one. The next day, father superior Moses led the burial service in the presence of all the brethren. Friends of Paul shed some tears on the separation from the unforgettable brother, but every monk present thanked God that he had vouchsafed the deceased such a peaceful Christian death and wished that the Lord would grant him the same death. Later Hermogenes, the cousin of the deceased, asked Father Leo to tell him about the inner virtues of Paul, but Father Leo told him just that: "Paul is great to God, and the Lord will glorify him."

Chapter 13. The last days of father Leo

Also, at an advanced age father Leo kept a cheerful spirit, and he never complained about his health. But his years and his huge workload took their toll. In 1841 he got a serious illness and his struggle with approaching death began. From the first days of September, he became noticeably weaker. But he did not accept any help from doctors as he put all his hope upon the Lord. In the last days of his life father Leo did not take any food, he nourished himself only with the holy Communion.

On September 15th he was administered the last rites and from that day he began to prepare for death. He said farewell to the brethren who visited him, he blessed them and left no one without consolation. On September 28th he received the holy Mysteries, he asked the canon for the departing soul to be sung. The brethren around him felt they were soon to become orphans and they pleaded him not to leave them without guidance. He was brought to tears, and he said: "Children! If I will gain the boldness from the Lord, I will care for all of you. Now I entrust you to the Lord. He will help you to finish this course of life, if only you resort to Him, He will save you from temptation."

On Saturday 24th October father Leo blessed all those around him and he said: "Now God's mercy will be with me." After these words his spirit rejoiced and although he experienced severe physical suffering, he could not hide his joy and his face brightened up. With a prayer on his lips father Leo gave up his spirit to God. On the third day, in the presence of a huge crowd, the funeral service for father Leo was held; the venerable spiritual mentor and priest was buried near the cathedral of the Presentation in the Temple, behind the side chapel of hierarch Nicholas the Wonderworker.

It was a comfort to the grieving that they could be confident that the father Leo was with the Lord and in glory. He himself described in one of his letters the life that awaits the righteous after death: "The Holy Scripture tells us that through death we are losing this life and that we gain a future life: eternal and painless. A life in which no passion disturbs us, no envy consumes us, no offences trouble us. A life that has no decrepit old age and no childhood weakness, but an ever-flowering state, not subject to any changes. That life is a blessed sojourn that has no limits, an immaculate life far from all worldly temptations."

Priest-monk Makarios, the faithful disciple of father Leo and his successor in spiritual mentorship, expressed the general feeling of the spiritual children of father Leo, "Our beloved father Leo is already not with us, his body is concealed from us by the damp mother earth, but his soul has departed right into the hands of God... I suppose you grieve about our orphanhood, but all together be consoled about the peace he shall undoubtedly find according to the mercy of God... It is impossible to doubt that he will be found worthy to receive the mercy of the Lord, and most likely he will intercede for us sinners, who are wandering in this vale of tears and who are struggling with our passions of soul and body."

* * *

www.ingramcontent.com/pod-product-compliance
Lightning Source LLC
LaVergne TN
LVHW041537070526
838199LV00046B/1698